stress reduction
for busy people

Other books in the Busy People series

Massage for Busy People
Meditation for Busy People
Yoga for Busy People

stress reduction
for busy people

Finding Peace in a Chronically Anxious World

Dawn Groves

New World Library
Novato, California

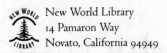

New World Library
14 Pamaron Way
Novato, California 94949

Front cover design by Mary Ann Casler
Text design and typography by Tona Pearce Myers

Library of Congress Cataloging-in-Publication Data
Groves, Dawn
  Stress reduction for busy people : finding peace in a chronically anxious world / Dawn Groves.
      p.   cm.
ISBN 1-57731-415-8 (pbk. : alk. paper)
1. Stress management. 2. Stress (Psychology)—Prevention.
3. Adjustment (Psychology) I. Title.
RA785.G768 2004
155.9'042—dc22   2003021840

First printing, February 2004
ISBN 1-57731-415-8
Printed in the U.S.A.
Distributed to the trade by Publishers Group West

10 9 8 7 6 5 4 3 2 1

To my dear husband, Dan, and our daughters, Holly and Samantha.
I love you from here to the moon and back.

contents

acknowledgments

I would first like to thank my editors, Carol Venolia and Alexander Slagg at New World Library for their solid contributions to the quality of this book. Especially I want to acknowledge editorial director Georgia Hughes for believing in me despite many setbacks, and for generously offering as much time as I needed to complete the manuscript. Thanks also to Mary Ann Casler and Tona Pearce Myers for design and typesetting.

In my persona life, I want to acknowledge Rev. Colleen MacGilchrist for her belief in my work and her idea for the title of the book; Tawni Gomes for reminding me that ordinary people can do extraordinary things; Peggie Collins at A Country Hideaway for creating the perfect setting to complete the manuscripts; and my circle of red-thread friends, Pat, Suzy, Jeanine, Jackie, Missy, Kathy, and Cindy, who continue to include me in their plans despite my tendency to fall asleep on the couch.

In my family I am grateful to my parents-in-law, Dan and Dorothy Barrett, for their unselfish help when things get tough. I also thank my daughter Holly for displaying patience beyond that of a typical seven-year-old. In re. ponse to the countless times she'd ask Daddy, "Isn't Mommy done with that book yet?" I can now reply, "Yes, Sweetie. I'm finally done."

Appreciation also goes to my younger daughter, Samantha, who by forcibly planting herself atop my papers and demanding, "Weed me a stow-wee," reminded me of what was most important in life. Then there's my husband, Dan, who shakes his head at my love/hate relationship with writing but still champions it and me. I am indeed a fortunate being.

introduction

When I first proposed this book idea to New World Library, I thought I'd passed life's big stress-management proficiency exam. After a series of trials with my health and work, I'd emerged triumphant and ready to share what I'd learned. I began writing with gusto.

Then everything fell apart.

My elderly mom had a stroke, forcing moves from apartment to hospital to nursing home. My husband's job became tenuous. Our two children (ages six and four) were feeling my absence while I tended to Mom. I stopped sleeping. I endured brutal headaches that made it difficult to perform my teaching job. We moved twice in four months. I developed severe plantar fasciitis in both feet, making it almost impossible to walk or stand for long periods. My bite shifted and I had jaw pain. I gained weight. A visit to the doctor confirmed that my blood pressure had skyrocketed. All this within an eight-month period — and I was in the middle of writing a book about stress reduction!

It exhausts me to remember that time. A monkey could have written better copy than I was generating. My stress-management routines were failing. I was only half present in every facet of my life. Finally, I stopped fighting and dropped headfirst into despair.

Dark nights of the soul aren't unfamiliar to me. At the turn of the millennium, I was diagnosed with cancer. I remember the core-level fear, the apprehension about my family's future, the "why-me" thinking. I also remember coming through that experience stronger, happier, and healthier than I had felt in a long time. So here it was again: loss of control, loneliness, physical pain. But this time the culprit wasn't cancer; it was chronic, toxic stress.

But I didn't die. I healed.

Today I still have an elderly mother with dementia, two active young daughters, a busy husband, and a career. My feet still bother me, but my blood pressure is normal. I no longer suffer debilitating headaches. My jaw is fine. I sleep well and I wake up smiling. My family is happy. I'm fifteen pounds lighter. I'm creative again. And, as you can see, I finished this book.

▲▲▲

Like the other Busy People books I've written, this book is designed to be practical, accessible, and easy to read quickly. It has only four chapters, and it concludes with a list of common questions that reference associated text in the book.

The first chapter talks about what the stress response is and what it does to the body. Stress has powerful physiological repercussions that can cascade into serious problems over time. When I woke up to how badly my body was being hurt by chronic anxiety, I committed myself to getting a handle on it. Hopefully this chapter will wake you up as well.

The second chapter talks about managing stress in the physical, mental/emotional, and spiritual realms. First, I'll describe specific practices to help you release the chemicals produced by the stress response, giving you physical relief and helping to circumvent the drain on your immune system. Then we'll look at how your attitude affects your health; mental/emotional outlook is the origin of most stress. I'll conclude the chapter with a discussion of spiritual practices such as meditation and prayer. These are tremendous coping resources, no matter what your religious persuasion.

The third chapter deals with handling crises. I've included a three-step approach that can help when you feel overwhelmed and unable to respond effectively. I'll share some ideas on living in an age of fear, with global catastrophe and physical/emotional threats to our personal security. I'll conclude the chapter by suggesting ways to help children deal with everyday stress and national catastrophes.

The fourth chapter is devoted to a process I find particularly useful for managing the stresses of living: spiritual goal-setting. I'm a big believer in setting and achieving goals as a life-management practice, but I also think that stress disappears when we stop fixating on achievement and find peace within our current circumstances. Achieving a goal and releasing attachment to it are important skills to have in a rapidly changing world. This chapter also addresses common excuses for not setting goals, offering a spiritual point of view.

At the end of the book I've provided a list of books that I highly recommend; each is a treasure trove.

▲▲▲

I'm not exceptional. I rail against life's unfairness as much as the next person. But I've found peaceful coexistence with this chronically anxious world — and if I can do it, you can do it. No matter how awful your circumstances, no matter how emotionally fried you think you are, there's a way to come through it with your health, your sanity, and your relationships intact. You can limit your stress response, find purpose within your suffering, take action to shift events or your perceptions of them, and open your mind to happiness despite current circumstances.

I am reminded of a quote from Henry Ward Beecher: "Tears are often the telescope by which men see far into heaven." Our tears can blind us or they can awaken us. Since they're already here, we might as well make good use of them. No, it's not always easy. You'll need to make a few course corrections. So what? Small changes reap big rewards when it comes to stress management. You can do this. Do you have any other choice?

1

understanding stress

The word "stress" conjures up a variety of unpleasant images: workaholism, muscle pain, exhaustion, short temper, sleeplessness. But stress itself isn't bad; it's normal. Life is full of positive and negative stressors (events that exert physical or emotional pressure), and the good news is that our bodies are well equipped to handle them. In a perfect world, we gear up emotionally and physically to deal with an event, and once it passes we return to business as usual.

Well, that's how it's supposed to work. But you and I know it doesn't happen like that anymore. Today's negative stressors are often long-term, subtle, and subjective. Issues such as eldercare, childcare, job insecurity, health, finances, information overload, personal safety, and now homeland security have no clear resolution and no apparent conclusion. They just lurk in the back of your mind, leaving you bewildered, edgy, and paranoid. Many of us almost never return to "business as usual."

We're Designed to Respond

How we process stress as individuals depends on a variety of factors, including how we've handled stress in the past, our genes (some people inherit a shorter fuse), our age, our socioeconomic background, our sex, the nature of the stressors, and how many stressors are occurring simultaneously. But the biology of the stress response is the same for all of us.

When you're frightened or alarmed, the stress response — also known as the fight-or-flight reaction — instantly kicks in. A cascade of chemical messengers (hormones, neurotransmitters, and amino acids) hurls you into a physiological and psychological condition known as "hyperarousal." This condition is triggered by the pituitary gland, which is located deep in the brain. It releases adrenocorticoid, a hormone that tells the adrenal glands to secrete epinephrine (also known as adrenaline), and cortisol. These two master stress hormones help rev up your body in the following ways:

- the pupils dilate
- the palms sweat
- breathing becomes shallow and fast
- the hair rises
- the heart beats faster and harder
- blood pressure shoots up
- digestion shuts down
- insulin surges into the bloodstream
- blood flow (oxygen) is redirected to the large muscles of the body
- the brain receives extra oxygen and blood

This impressive process is managed by the autonomic nervous system (ANS), which in turn is controlled by the hypothalamus — a central area on the underside of the brain that regulates the body's involuntary functions. The ANS has two branches: sympathetic and parasympathetic. The sympathetic branch is what speeds you up; the parasympathetic branch slows you down. The sympathetic branch kicks in when you're threatened; the parasympathetic branch returns you to normal after the threat passes.

The problem is that your brain's hypothalamus can't distinguish between a real threat and an imagined threat. It bases its unconscious response on the *perception* of threat or danger. For example, if you're afraid of mice, the hypothalamus will jump-start your stress response whenever you see a mouse, despite the fact that it poses no real danger. Someone whose perception of mice is more neutral will have an entirely different response to them. The hypothalamus can be triggered by social fears as easily as it can by a genuine physical threat. This unconscious triggering can then expand into benign situations, such as a business meeting. To the hypothalamus, any fear is a legitimate stressor.

The automatic, unconscious triggering of the fight-or-flight reaction is useful if we are dealing with dangerous or unpredictable circumstances. A hormonal rush of strength prepares us to do battle or to run like hell; either choice appropriately exhausts our body, allowing our heart to stop pounding, our blood pressure to calm down, and our muscles to recuperate.

If, however, the rush comes when we're in a non-threatening situation — such as at a party — then there's nowhere to run, and we're forced to suppress what we're feeling. The body is in hyperarousal, but since we're not doing anything about it, our muscular, skeletal, nervous, gastrointestinal, and emotional systems absorb the tension. The more often our stress response is triggered, the more our insides take the hit and roil with anxiety. Eventually our bodies become habituated to living in high gear. We grow accustomed to back pain, heartburn, emotional over-reactivity, and insomnia. At this point, hyperarousal is no longer a discrete event from which we recover. Instead, it slowly breaks down our physical and emotional health. According to the National Institute of Mental Health, 75 to 90 percent of all doctor visits are prompted by stress-related concerns.

Don't Worry about It

We've become a culture of worriers. Psychiatrist Edward M. Hallowell, M.D., has written extensively about worry and its damaging effects. He defines excessive worry as "a heightened sense of vulnerability in the presence of a diminished feeling of power and control."[2] You can exhaust yourself by worrying about something all day, never taking any real action to solve the problem. The more helpless you feel, the greater your apprehension. The greater your apprehension, the less energy you have to take action, and the more helpless you feel. It's a vicious cycle.

Because worry is based in fear, the body registers it as a threat and the hypothalamus triggers the stress response. In the case of ongoing worry, the adrenals just keep on secreting varying levels of epinephrine and cortisol in preparation for a battle that never happens. Muscles live in contraction. Blood pressure goes up and stays up.

The Good, the Bad, and the Ugly

As with everything else on earth, the stress response has good and bad aspects. We evolved this intricate protective response system to help us survive in a harsh, wild environment. But modern society doesn't require the same kinds of responses. The stress response is still useful, but "stand and fight" or "run like hell" are no longer our only two choices.

The Good

Not all stressors are created equal; many emerge from happy occasions. There's the stress of getting married, taking a vacation, riding a roller coaster, or moving into a nice new house. The term for this kind of good stress is "eustress." Happy stressors stimulate the sympathetic nervous system, just like scary ones, but the pleasurable nature of the circumstances tends to keep the response manageable and even gratifying. Butterflies in one's stomach are perceived as thrilling instead of uncomfortable. When it comes to stress, perception is everything.

The stress response isn't a monster; in its proper context, it supports and protects us. It helps our bodies adapt to changes in the environment, and adaptation and growth are the harbingers of longevity. Without adaptation, the human species would have died out long ago.

Stress of any kind also gives us energy and focus as the surge of insulin fuels the brain. If you're giving a speech or conducting an interview, the adrenalin can make you glow with vibrancy. Increased mental acuity helps you strategize on the fly. The stress response often provides the winning edge in sports competitions. Students use the stress of an exam deadline to motivate them to study. And don't forget those everyday stories of stress-induced heroism, such as a mother lifting a car to free her child pinned beneath it. There are countless healthy applications for hyperarousal.

The Bad

The Buddha talked about moderation in all things, and this certainly applies to the stress response. On occasion it is useful, but when it becomes chronic it is terribly damaging to the body. There is ample evidence of the role of stress in gastrointestinal, dermatological, respiratory, neurological, and emotional ailments, as well as proof of its impact on a wide range of disorders linked to immune-system disturbances, from the common cold to herpes and arthritis. A 1998 study by the National Institute for Occupational Safety and Health found that

> When stressful situations go unresolved, the body is kept in a constant state of activation, which increases the rate of wear and tear to biological systems. Ultimately, fatigue or damage results, and the ability of the body to repair and defend itself can become seriously compromised. As a result, the risk of injury or disease escalates.[3]

Here is a short list of physical troubles related to chronic stress:

- Sleep disturbances increase in number and severity;

- immune-system antibodies are suppressed, increasing the risk of bacterial infections, susceptibility to viruses, and perhaps even the likelihood of developing cancer;

- respiratory problems increase, especially asthma;

- gastrointestinal problems develop or worsen, often contributing to debilitating conditions such as Crohn's disease;

- increased insulin levels cause fat to be deposited around the middle of the body, leading to increased risk of heart attack, insulin resistance, and diabetes;

- high blood pressure and higher cholesterol levels increase the risk of heart disease, as well as the possibility of stroke;

- excessive tension in the jaw area can cause bite problems and headaches;

- back and neck problems are often caused or exacerbated by unrelieved muscle strain.

The above list doesn't take into account the perils of what pioneer stress researcher Hans Selye termed "diseases of adaptation."[4] That is, the manner in which we cope with stress can be more damaging than the stress response itself. Stress, many people turn to drugs, smoking, overeating, acting out, or a combination of disruptive, harmful behaviors. Any of these can spawn their own pantheon of problems.

Chronic unnecessary worry is called Generalized Anxiety Disorder. As noted in the publication "Facts about Anxiety Disorders,"[5] available from The National Institute of Mental Health, anxiety disorders as a group are now the most commonly diagnosed mental illness in America. Anxiety is insidious because the shallow breathing that accompanies it doesn't allow enough oxygen into the body. Your brain then tells you that you're suffering from oxygen deprivation, which causes more anxiety. You begin to breathe harder, which can generate hyperventilation and panic. It's difficult to slow down your breath when you're in the middle of anxiety-induced rapid breathing.

Without a doubt, too much stress ages you, sickens you, and, as you'll read below, ruins your outlook.

The Ugly

It's difficult to be cheerful or hopeful when you're carrying more than your fair share of stress. Even the happiest of individuals will feel exhausted by the end of a highly stressful day. You stop relating to family members as partners in life, instead seeing them as just another set of obligations. This behavior quickly becomes habitual, eroding the very relationships that are supposed to support you. You can become sour and unpleasant. Even worse, you may adjust to the discomfort, hobbling around in denial until you lose touch with your family, your friends, and eventually your health. Stress doesn't just make you sick; it makes you lonely.

Chronic stress doesn't necessarily turn life into a black hole, but it can surely suck color from the world. It wears down the psyche. It robs us of our creative energy and results in a condition known as "burnout." A person suffering from burnout either looks like a raging bull or a deer in the headlights. Neither appearance is encouraging.

Why It's Hard to Calm Down

The American Dream isn't what it used to be. Life's stressors seem to have a greater influence on us. Our supportive structures of yesteryear — the nuclear family and the close-knit community — have been eroding. Children define themselves, not by their family's standards, but by the sitcom standards of television actors. Too much emphasis on external reinforcement, such as clothes and appearance, leads to insecurity and a relentless search for approval. We need to craft a new dream — one that places value on our dignity, our compassion, our good works, our mindful intelligence, and our moral character.

We Suppress Our Feelings

There is clear evidence that suppressing emotional expression may play a role in hypertension and cancer. People who habitually express their anger when provoked by others have lower average blood pressures than people who habitually suppress such feelings. In high-stress situations, the ability to vent one's feelings is protective. Even tears are useful; crying rids your body of excess cortisol with every teardrop.

Regrettably, Western culture values emotional containment, not expression. People who can "keep it together" are respected. Showing too much emotion is often deemed unseemly or undisciplined. As a result, communication is thwarted. Thoughts and feelings are railroaded into our arteries, muscles, soft tissues, and immune system. It's a no-win situation and a one-way road to misunderstanding.

We Overrate Productivity

Our society defines success by how much work we generate or how much money we earn. If you're not rich, you'd better be productive. It's the puritan work ethic on steroids, and it's eroding our quality of life. Too much leisure is considered lazy. Certainly we all want to be contributing members of society, but in order to be productive we need some downtime. Leisure is not lazy; it's necessary. Creativity and happiness come from having room to breathe.

We Isolate Ourselves

Human beings are naturally social; we're meant to find safety and pleasure by being together. But in the last thirty years we've become seriously isolated, both as individuals and as a culture. As individuals, many of us substitute televised relationships for flesh-and-blood connections with our friends and family. More recently, the Internet has facilitated a social expansion that is often contrived and two-dimensional. Chat-room associations appease our need for connection without ever delivering any real human companionship. E-mail allows us to communicate without risk. Cybernetic conversations are carefully scripted, and many never progress beyond words on a screen.

As a culture, our isolation has inoculated us against the pain and struggle that most of humanity must endure on a daily basis. The result is that we are woefully out of touch with global concerns; the repercussions of this alienation are showing up in world opinion and politics.

We Compartmentalize Our Experience

Relaxation should be scheduled for weekends and during vacation. Family bonding should happen at the dinner table and during planned evening activities. Recuperation should occur during sleep. What's wrong with this picture?

Musician John Lennon wrote that life is what happens while you're busy making other plans. He'd probably agree that relaxation, renewal, and recuperation don't always show up on a timeline. Neither does bonding, for that matter. Without room for give-and-take, without embracing the natural messiness of life, we set ourselves up for disappointment and repeated failure. We squelch the very things that give us juice: serendipity, surprise, revelation.

We Don't Know How to Relax

People who need to relax often enroll in classes that teach yoga, biofeedback, and meditation. We need to be taught because most of us can't simply sink back into a chair, close our eyes, sigh, and let the world melt away. Our bodies are so keyed up, our worlds so busy, our lists so full, that becoming quiet is about as realistic as flying to the moon — and just about as easy. A chronically anxious person doesn't know what it feels like to be calm. Fortunately for our bodies and our psyches, calmness can be learned. Properly executed relaxation exercises can relieve chronic stress and counteract the cascade of hormones that keep us on edge. Relaxing and quieting an overactive stress response is one of the most important commitments we can make to our health and sanity.

We Watch Too Much Television

Some studies estimate that, in the average American household, the television is on seven hours a day. Being bombarded with information, graphic images, and sounds without letup can generate enormous unconscious stress. Television agitates us, making it harder to think clearly or relax completely. It robs us of time for other activities that feed personal connections. It influences every aspect of our lives: our standards of desirability, our political opinions, our dreams, our ethics, and our behavior.

Children often spend more time in front of the television than they spend doing anything else except sleeping. The American Academy of Pediatrics recommends that children over the age of two be limited to one or two hours of television per day. Because it negatively affects their brain development, children under age two shouldn't watch television at all. According to LimiTV (www.limitv.org), a nonprofit North Carolina corporation formed to educate parents, teachers, and children about the problems of excessive television viewing, too much television slows the development of thinking skills and imagination in children. It also shortens their attention spans and slows the growth of their reading and speaking skills.

We Have No Time to Spare

It's a cliché that we have too many projects and too little time to enjoy them. But the stress damage that results from constantly rushing from one project to the next is no cliché. We're trying to do too much, and our health, our happiness, and our passion for life are suffering. We somehow believe that if we can just fit everything in, we'll be happy. It's an unwholesome message to give ourselves, and an even worse one to communicate to our children.

The idea that we don't have enough time to accomplish everything we want to do is absurd. We all have the same twenty-four hours, but some of us use them more intelligently than others. The problem usually isn't lack of time; it's lack of focus. We're running in too many directions and scattering our energy. We need to properly select a few important projects and focus on them alone. Proper selection is the key. This leaves us room to enjoy our efforts and time for some spontaneity. (See chapter 4, "Spiritual Goal-Setting.")

Rushing through life sabotages any hope of happiness. Life happens now, not later when the list of tasks is completed. Happiness happens in the present moment. Finding peace requires paying attention and slowing down. Haste rarely results in satisfaction. Jon Kabat-Zinn, founder of the Stress Reduction Clinic at the University of Massachusetts Medical Center, says it better than anyone else: "Inner peace exists outside of time."[6]

▲▲▲

The purpose of this book is not to add stress management as another "have-to" on your already full to-do list. Instead, we'll look at the problems created by chronic stress, and I'll introduce a series of mental, physical, and spiritual behavioral changes that can help relieve your stress burden. Try them; see which suggestions work for you. Many of these changes may seem small. However, as they accumulate you will find yourself breathing more easily and smiling more often. Good luck!

2

....

managing stress in
body, mind, and spirit

Life doesn't have to be a process of ongoing damage control. There are many things we can do to keep stress from eroding our health and happiness. In this chapter, I'll cover strategies for stress management on a purely physical level, then I'll conclude with some ideas about emotional and spiritual support. You'll notice that some of these suggestions are easy to implement, while others may challenge aspects of your lifestyle. You may need to ask yourself how bad things have to get before you'll put your health first.

The fastest way to fix the problems in your life is to remove your stressors. It's also the hardest. But don't worry; there are alternatives to firing your boss, leaving your home, redesigning your spouse, or trading in your body. You've been hearing about these alternatives for years; now it's time to take them seriously:

- Get enough sleep.

- Eat healthful foods.

- Exercise regularly.

Consider approaching this information with what Buddhists call a "beginner's mind." A beginner's mind looks at old material with new eyes. It consciously sets aside the jaded, sophisticated, often cynical mind-set that dampens enthusiasm and devalues the tried and true. A beginner's mind is open at the top. It still believes in miracles. It says, "Okay, maybe there's more to this. Maybe there's something I've missed."

It may be hard to create a beginner's mind in relation to the purely physical issues of getting more sleep, eating healthful food, and exercising regularly. They're frequently mentioned in just about every magazine printed. We know they're important. So why don't we actually do them?

- *We don't like old news.* Our mothers told us to do these things when we were children. Most of us would prefer something more exotic or entertaining.

- *We're impatient.* We don't want to work with nature; we're used to jumping over it. Healthful sleeping, eating, and exercise practices work in harmony with nature. Their benefits take time to manifest.

- *We think that "difficult" means "wrong."* If a project requires too much effort, or if we meet with obstacles along the way, we think the project must not be right for us. We've forgotten that people almost always encounter resistance when they move in new directions. Almost everything easy was hard at one time.

- *We're always waiting for the perfect time.* The perfect time doesn't arrive on a white stallion; it is generated as we face up to our challenges. Waiting only begets more waiting. Action begets action.

- *We're tired of self-improvement.* We're overwhelmed by the extent of our imperfections

and often give up before we start. Some of
us have successfully changed a few habits;
we want that to be enough.

Changing your lifestyle takes effort, but it isn't impossible. Lots of people have done it — people with bigger
problems and fewer resources than you. There's an old
saying: How you do one thing is how you do everything. I
would add to that: If you change how you do one thing,
you change how you do everything. Each change makes
the next one easier. Noble projects have a positive ripple
effect in your life and in the lives of those around you.

Sometimes my daughter looks up from doing her
homework and complains, "Momma, it's so hard." I
tell her, "You can do hard." My response comes from
author Bo Lozoff, director and cofounder of the
Human Kindness Foundation and its award-winning
Prison Ashram Project.[7] "Hard" isn't the enemy. It feels
good to complete something hard. "Hard" doesn't have
to stop her — or you.

Get Enough Sleep

Despite our being inundated with timesaving technolo-
gies, the last twenty years have seen ten hours added to

the average workweek. Since there are still only twenty-four hours in a day — and they are already booked up — the easiest place to grab time is from sleep.

According to the National Sleep Foundation (www.sleepfoundation.org), most adults need an average of eight hours of sleep; however, some can function without drowsiness with as little as six, while others may require up to ten. During sleep, chemicals important to the immune system are secreted. The National Institute for Neurological Disorders and Stroke (www.ninds.nih.gov/health_and_medical/pubs/understanding_sleep_brain_basic_htm) states,

> Some experts believe sleep gives neurons used while we are awake a chance to shut down and repair themselves. Without sleep, neurons may become so depleted in energy or so polluted with byproducts of normal cellular activities that they begin to malfunction. Sleep also may give the brain a chance to exercise important neuronal connections that might otherwise deteriorate from lack of activity.

This suggests that sleep gives the body a chance to repair itself. It may be a way of recharging the brain, readying it for another day's work. Many cells increase production and reduce breakdown of proteins during deep sleep. Proteins are the building blocks needed for cell growth and for repair of damage from stress and ultraviolet rays.

However, a study conducted by Dr. David Dinges at the Institute of Pennsylvania Hospital and the University of Pennsylvania in Philadelphia found that after two weeks of chronic sleep loss, participants were clearly impaired by fatigue despite the fact that they believed they had adapted well.[8] Everything they did took longer to accomplish. This tells us that, even though we think subjectively that we do fine with less sleep, objectively we're likely to be underperforming.

The wear and tear of exhaustion eventually becomes evident in everyone, although older bodies break down faster. Problems can include memory impairment, a weakened immune system, mental fogginess, hormonal imbalance, and an inability to remain emotionally stable. Prolonged sleep deprivation can alter metabolic and endocrine function to the extent that it mimics aging. Shortened nights also cause blood glucose levels to rise, generating an influx of insulin. Unchecked insulin resistance can lead to weight gain and diabetes.

The ability to sleep, rather than the need for sleep,

appears to decrease with advancing age. Young people enjoy deep sleep — the most restful kind — for up to one hundred minutes each night. If they shorten their sleeping time, they can make up for the loss of deep sleep on subsequent evenings. Middle-aged people only average twenty minutes of deep sleep per night. That's why, when middle-aged people become sleep-deprived, they may not be able to compensate for it as easily.

One of the most common first symptoms of too much stress is insomnia: poor-quality sleep, difficulty falling asleep, waking up frequently with trouble returning to sleep, or awakening unrefreshed. That's because sleep isn't generated or forced; it is allowed. Sleep is a form of surrender. The last thing a stressed-out mind wants to do is let go.

If you have trouble sleeping, talk with your doctor to rule out the possibility of a physiological cause. Here are a few suggestions to help regenerate a healthy sleep cycle:

- Establish a regular aerobic exercise routine. The common explanation for how exercise helps promote sleep is that the body recognizes its need to conserve energy and restore itself after the day's activities. Vigorous exercise should be timed at least five or six hours before bedtime to help the body cool down.

- Don't drink, smoke, or eat before bed. You may also need to cut back on caffeine in general.

- Avoid taking naps. People without sleep problems can benefit from brief naps, says Dr. James Maas, a psychologist at Cornell University and the author of *Power Sleep*.[9] However, people who have trouble falling asleep at night should avoid them.

- Instead of tossing and turning, get up and do tai chi or yoga. The gentle, deep breathing that accompanies this kind of exercise can help reduce tension, making it easier to fall asleep when you return to bed.

- Wear socks or warm your feet with a hot water bottle. The body appears to prepare for sleep by widening the blood vessels in the hands and feet to help radiate away body heat. Warming the feet promotes this dilation, possibly encouraging the body to settle down.

- Recondition yourself to associate your bed only with sleep. That means no reading in bed.

- Go to bed and arise at consistent times. Habit is a great helpmate when it comes to falling asleep. We feel hungry on schedule. We can also condition ourselves to feel sleepy on schedule.

- Perform a full-body relaxation. Do a progressive relaxation process by inhaling while tensing your foot muscles, then exhaling and relaxing them. Next, inhale while tightening your calves and ankles; exhale and relax them. Continue in this manner, slowly working all the way up to the top of your head. Take more time to exhale than to inhale.

- Consider working with a hypnotherapist to help you learn to relax and drop off to sleep.

Eat Healthful Foods

The body wants food for one reason only: fuel. If we all listened to our bodies, we'd never have a problem with nutrition or weight. Unfortunately, our minds are usually in charge of deciding when to eat. Our "appetite" is triggered by pictures, smells, memories, time of day, fatigue, comfort needs, avoidance rituals, boredom, and, of course, stress. Stress plays havoc with established eating patterns. Anxiety encourages unconscious nibbling, eating too fast, bingeing, and eating for distraction.

The stress response not only affects how much and how often we eat; it also affects what we want to eat. Sugar, caffeine, and high-fat snacks, with their strong flavors and pungent aromas, offer quick distraction and a brief surge of energy. Sadly, the energy is short-lived because these foods typically pack little nutritional punch. If the body keeps craving nutrients and the mind keeps responding with convenience foods, it generates a vicious cycle that is a setup for overeating. The National Institutes of Health (www.nih.gov) puts the number of overweight adults in the United States at 60 percent of our population — and growing.

Vitamins may help. High-stress vitamin formulations emphasize B-vitamins, which marshal fuel sources in the blood. Vitamin B6 helps the brain produce serotonin, which may reduce psychological stress. Vitamin C supports the adrenal glands. However, the American Dietetic Association (www.eatright.org) postulates that stress alone doesn't generate a physical need for vitamin supplements; it is the poor eating habits resulting from stress that can deplete us. The stress response also slows digestion, increasing the length of time it takes for nutrients to enter our system.

Herbs are often recommended as stress-reduction supplements. Kava kava is suggested as a way to calm down and fall asleep more easily. Valerian, hops, and passionflower are said to reduce nervousness and anxiety. Peppermint tea aids digestion. Some research suggests that taking ginseng improves mental performance and enhances the body's ability to deal with stress. However, ginseng is a stimulant and shouldn't be taken before bed. (Those who are pregnant or breastfeeding, or who have high blood pressure, shouldn't take ginseng at all.) Herbs can be powerful. Always consult a dietician or healthcare provider before embarking on an herbal or vitamin regimen.

Supplements and herbs can support a healthy lifestyle. However, there is no substitute for balanced eating. Eating healthful food is even more important during times of stress, when your body's nutrient supplies are depleted and your immune system becomes weakened. You don't want to stack nutritional deficit on top of hyperarousal. Life is challenging enough as it is.

If you're a stress eater, I have a one-word solution

for you: plan. Planning makes all the difference. When you plan ahead and have healthful, nutritious snacks within easy reach, you're more likely to avoid consuming empty calories. Because the appeal of convenience foods is often their availability, you should stock your pantry with bags of precut vegetables, fruits, and whole-grain crackers. Healthy snacks satisfy your body, lessening the drive for continual nibbling. Fresh water is also a good, filling snack; thirst is often mistaken for hunger.

Although planning is a great strategy, overplanning can generate its own anxiety state. Try not to demand too much of yourself during times of pressure. For example, I don't expect myself to plan an entire week's worth of meals when I am rushed. Instead, I look at the next couple of days and arrange a few easy meals to get me through. Sometimes I wake up in the morning and say to myself, "Okay, I know this is going to be a tough afternoon. What can I set aside to avoid sugar binges?" Ten minutes of preparation can make a big difference in the long run.

If possible, try to determine what you're really craving. Listen to your body. Do you want food, or do you want understanding? Food, or security? Do you want the taste of a particular food, or do you want the experience of satiation? A taste craving can be satisfied with just a couple of bites. If you're looking for satiation — that feeling of being full — then consider filling up on fruit salad or whole-grain cereal instead of potato chips. And if physical hunger isn't the problem, food is never going to be the answer.

Eat foods in combination to boost nutritional intake, maximize emotional/physical satisfaction, and decrease the drive to snack. Try for something that contains protein (dairy products, beans, meat) along with fruits, vegetables, and whole-grain bread. Add a little fat to help it stick with you for a while. I'm a big fan of convenience, so I'll often grab yogurt, an apple, and a whole-grain roll or maybe a peanut-butter sandwich. They're fast, easy, portable, and very satisfying. Soups, stews, and salads are quick and tasty options, too.

When times get tough, try power-grazing six small meals instead of three big ones. Keep your food choices smart. Your blood-sugar level will remain steady (no energy belly flops), you won't be hungry, and you'll avoid the lethargy that comes from eating too much at one sitting.

Try "skinnying" your other foods to compensate for the extra calories you may consume during times of stress. Use egg substitute instead of eggs. Cut your use of oil in half. Use nonfat or low-fat dairy substitutes. If you bake, use applesauce instead of oil (a one-for-one exchange; it works!) and cut the sugar content by up to one-third. You don't want to add weight gain to your list of stressors.

If losing weight is important to you, try not to begin a weight-loss program when your life is crazy. I realize that life is always crazy for some of us (if I waited until circumstances were perfect, I've never attempt anything new). However, there is a natural ebb and flow to even the busiest of lives. If you consider how you're feeling, then look at your schedule objectively, you can probably determine whether now is the best time to add weight loss to your list of challenges. It might be better to focus on health maintenance. Weight loss can come later.

Exercise Regularly

Almost everyone needs more exercise. This isn't news. What is news is the connection between exercise and our ability to manage stress, both mentally and physically.

The popular theory that exercise causes a feel-good rush of endorphins is still being researched. However, according to the American Council on Exercise (www.acefitness.org), one exercise session can generate from 90 to 120 minutes of "endorphin response." For example, recent studies have shown that when large muscle groups repeatedly contract and relax, the brain receives a signal to release specific neurotransmitters, which in turn help us feel calmer and more alert. Exercise also appears to decrease the buildup of the stress hormone cortisol. High levels of cortisol are linked to everything from immune-system dysfunction to osteoporosis and arthritis. Exercise may increase the level of norepinephrine in the blood, which may help the brain handle stress more efficiently.

I like to think of exercise as my neurotransmitter elixir. Before I work out, I'm usually resistant and burdened; the committee in my head screams that I should be doing something else with my time. Thirty minutes later — even after the crummiest, least inspired workout possible (I do have those days) — I feel taller, energized, more relaxed and focused, and relieved that, once again, I put my health first. Committee: 0. Me: 1. Perhaps most important, when I leave the gym or the pool or the park, I feel hopeful. It isn't just my body that's changed; it's also my mind.

Another theory that's gaining acceptance is that

exercise gives your body a chance to practice dealing with stress — to get better at handling it. If you become weakened through sedentary living, illness, or injury, your cardiovascular, renal, muscular, and nervous systems are less efficient when responding to stress. Stressors in your life can punch harder and hurt more. Regular exercise, on the other hand, forces your body's functional systems to communicate more closely than usual. It gives them a kind of shakedown, and the result is improved management of the stress response. Your body can become more stress-hardy.

The exercise technique that best provides stress-hardiness training is called "interval exercise." In this approach, the heart is taxed for short periods of time in a series of exercise intervals. Properly executed, interval exercise generates a high stress response, followed by a period of recovery. (For example, one minute of high-intensity exercise followed by two minutes of easy recovery. See page 44 for more information.) Interval exercise is designed to mimic and exaggerate the ups and downs of stress in life. It trains the body and mind to bounce back from sudden stressors that appear in the normal course of living.

With today's unholy mix of fast food, sedentary jobs, and moving walkways, exercise really isn't optional.

If you have a body and you want to keep it, you must exercise it. Review the following list and see if you don't become inspired to give exercise another try:

- Physical exercise bathes the body with stress-reducing neurotransmitters.

- Exercise can help reduce the pain and joint damage caused by arthritis.

- Exercise decreases the need for medication in asthma sufferers.

- Many people believe that exercise in combination with other helpful lifestyle changes may slow the progress of cancer.

- Regular exercise eases anxiety and depression, often lessening the need for medication.

- Exercise makes you look and feel better.

- Some research suggests that regular workouts may cut the risk of gallstones.

- Recent research suggests that exercise can reduce the side effects of chemotherapy.

- Exercise reduces the heart rate and therefore decreases the risk of cardiovascular disease.

- Exercise reduces the bone loss associated with age or osteoporosis.

- Exercise increases the basal metabolic rate (BMR) by approximately 10 percent. The BMR is the rate at which calories are burned by your body when you are at rest. The higher your BMR, the more fuel you burn even when sedentary.

- Exercise reduces your appetite. Most people are less hungry after they exercise, particularly if the exercise is moderate to vigorous.

- Exercise helps prevent the snowball effect in conditions such as diabetes.

- Exercise increases your sense of control, helping ease the physical and emotional fallout associated with helplessness.

- Exercise is an emotional release valve. It's a way to vent anger and frustration — mental states that block logical thinking and inhibit problem-solving.

Yes, exercise is one more "should" to add to your already overflowing list of responsibilities. Maybe you feel you don't have time to fit it in. Maybe you don't like to exercise. You don't have the proper attire. You can't afford it. You don't have anyone to watch the kids. You're too tired, sick, old, busy, et cetera. There are a thousand reasons not to start an exercise program. But let's be honest: each of these reasons, valid as it may seem, boils down to an excuse.

Consider Tawni Gomes's story. Five years ago, Tawni was 100 pounds overweight and in a wheelchair. Today she has completed countless marathons, has written a book about her experience, and speaks on topics of health and exercise while maintaining a full-time career. She runs an international support group called Connecting Connectors from her website (www.connectingconnectors.com), inspiring thousands of people with her daily e-mails. Tawni didn't like to exercise. She didn't have time to exercise. She did it anyway. Her motto: "No more excuses."

If you're not an exercise buff, this probably isn't going to be easy. I don't know of anyone who suddenly thought, "Gosh, I have two free hours in the morning. Maybe I'll start an exercise program." You'll have to force it for a while. The trick is to force it in small amounts. (Walk for ten minutes instead of thirty minutes, and build up to longer walks.) Once you start making room in your schedule, time will naturally begin to open up. The opening may not reveal itself right away, but it will come; your sincere intention will create it. Most of the effort is in the beginning. Starting an exercise program is like growing flowers in a field. Once the space is cleared and the seeds are planted, upkeep and maintenance are easy.

The secret to sticking to an exercise program is the same as the secret to sticking to a healthful eating program: planning. Planning has rescued me more times than I can count. When I wake up in the morning, I'm immediately pressed with demands on my energy and attention. My mental committee convinces me that I deserve to stay in bed for a few precious minutes. But I already have my clothes laid out, gym bag packed, and water bottle ready. My tea is prepared from the night before. It takes minimal effort for me to roll out of bed and get going. If I didn't have everything ready and waiting by the door, the committee would win.

Here are a few other suggestions to get you up and moving:

- *Do it first.* Yes, you may have good reasons to wait until the end of the day: you're not an early morning person, or your only free time is at night. However, if you are resistant to doing exercise, putting if off until the end of the day won't work. Your busy world will inundate even the best intentions. Do it first, or it just won't get done.

- *Do something different.* I've started countless get-in-shape programs, and the one that really took root was the one that was different: swimming. I never in a million years thought I'd swim. However, when both of my arches broke down with plantar fasciitis, the physical therapist said I had to do something. So I worked up my courage and bought a classic "big black swimsuit." I laid the swimsuit on the floor, sizing it up like an enemy. My first trip to the pool was daunting. I cajoled myself out of the dressing room with the mantra "Nobody's looking at me, nobody's looking at me..." But at first splash, I knew I'd done the right thing. It was heavenly. Today I'm swimming three and four times a week without fail. And, thank goodness, there's still nobody looking at me.

Doing something different gives you a temporary blast of energy. It shakes you out of complacency and that self-defeating feeling of "been there, done that." It ignites a little fear because it pushes you against your growing edge. There's juice in that fear. It can propel you into a new habit. That habit then carries you through tough times when motivation is low or commitment feels tenuous.

- *Keep a record.* It's easy for the mind to discount what you've accomplished. Western culture values big, sweeping changes; little ones are often ignored. Yet most changes are built on a series of small, committed actions. A record is an objective account of those actions. The mind can't refute them. There's something emotionally gratifying in a visual record, and that gratification fuels your commitment. Even better, it fuels your vision of yourself as a success.

- *Find a mentor.* Identify with someone who is doing what you want to do. If possible, find someone who overcame similar obstacles. Become a student of their success. It's too easy to separate yourself from others by believing that they are somehow different, gifted, blessed with qualities you don't have. Not true. When you dig beneath the surface, most successful people have trials and tribulations. Thinking that you can't measure up is just an excuse to quit.

- *Envision success.* What you dwell on, you empower in your life. Energy follows attention. Use this law to your advantage by filling your mind with success stories. Look for success stories in the library, and search the Internet for discussion groups that can support you.

- *Watch your words.* It doesn't matter how much "can-do" propaganda you read; if you continue to describe yourself as undisciplined or unsuccessful, your world will support that conclusion. Changing your world by changing your self-talk isn't hocus-pocus; it's a powerful tool used in competitive sports, public speaking, acting, and a host of other occupations. Cognitive therapists use positive self-talk as a tool to work through anxiety disorders, depression, and other negative states of mind.

When I decided to become physically active, I used positive self-talk by referring to myself as an active person. I'd joke with my friends, "I'm going to walk to the grocery store because that's what active people do." We'd all laugh, especially since I was about as inactive as a person could get without being dead. But I kept saying it and taking small steps, and pretty soon I actually became an active person. Today I still say it. I still smile about it. But I exercise regularly and I feel better than I've felt in years.

• *Do what you can.* Stretch within your limits. If you can't walk, maybe you can swim. If you can't swim, maybe you can bike or mow the lawn more often. If you can't lift your arm, then move your fingers. Never devalue what is currently possible for you to do. Always reinforce your growing edge.

Now that you're convinced that you must get serious about exercising, let's discuss which exercises to do.

There are basically two forms of exercise that best relieve day-to-day stress:

1. relaxation exercises, and

2. shakedown exercises.

Relaxation Exercises

Certain types of exercise work by directly inhibiting the stress response. They help teach the body and mind how to relax by diverting attention to breathing or moving slowly, carefully, and with control. This can lower heart rate and blood pressure, dissipating the stress chemicals and inducing relaxation and feelings of well-being. Examples of relaxation exercises are yoga, tai chi, and other practices that emphasize deliberate, mindful concentration on movement, alignment, and breathing. Walking, easy cycling, and other popular aerobic activities can also induce a calming response when they are performed rhythmically and mindfully.

Shakedown Exercises

Vigorous exercise also relieves stress. It generates healthy exhaustion, flushes anxiety, and helps you forget about your problems. Running, fast cycling, heavy weight lifting, sprint training, hard swimming, race-walking, cross-country skiing, and similar exercises all push your major muscle groups, your heart, and your lungs to capacity. The duration and intensity of the exercise can gradually be increased as your body adjusts, allowing for sufficient rest time between workouts.

Interval training fits into the shakedown category. On a treadmill, you could run hard for one minute and recover with a slow jog for two minutes, repeating the cycle for about twenty minutes. The same formula applies to deep-water runners. If you're walking out-doors, try power-walking up a hill to increase intensity, then take it easy going back down. What's important with interval training is to push hard and then take advantage of the recovery time during the slow interval. Remember, you're teaching your body to handle stress and recover from it quickly. Interval training can be applied to almost any aerobic activity.

A word about recovery. Exercise breaks down muscles; recovery allows them to repair. Strength and endurance result from the rebuilding that occurs during rest, after exercise is completed. The older you get, the more rest time you need. Try exercising different muscle groups on alternating days to give them a break. Take a day off from exercise each week — two days, if you're older. Vary your exercise routine to avoid over-training. Without sufficient rest time, your muscles don't repair and you become prone to injury.

Hard exercise also benefits your emotional state. After thirty minutes of deep breathing and full muscle engagement, you can think more clearly. Think of emotional stress as a windstorm caught inside your body. Physical movement gives it an outlet through your breathing and by working your big muscles. If you sit without moving, that windstorm can get trapped in your neck, your back, and your temples. If you try to eat it away, it can get trapped in your jaw, stomach, or intestines.

When you don't have a thirty-minute block of time to devote to exercise, try breaking your routine into two or three sessions throughout the day. An extended period of exercise is preferable, but short exercise breaks are also valuable. Don't be afraid to start small. If you can only do ten minutes of exercise, then try doing ten minutes a couple of times a day. Three sessions of ten minutes each burn the same number of calories as one thirty-minute session.

Your Stress-Management Strategy

I grew up in earthquake country: southern California. For weeks after an earthquake, everyone talked about The Big One that was destined to hit. I felt myself becoming stressed out about it. I knew I couldn't control earthquakes, so I'd have to find something I could control. I needed a strategy.

Strategies help you prevail in the face of stress. They help you take back your personal power. My strategy was twofold: 1) to demystify earthquakes by learning about them, and 2) to prepare an earthquake kit that included a few basics, extra water, and first-aid supplies. Once I strategized and took action, I felt much better. Earthquakes still made me nervous, but I wasn't powerless; I was proactive.

I think most people would agree that there are far worse things to fear than earthquakes. No matter where you look, something or someone is breaking down, getting sick, or growing angry. We live with countless threats, and our bodies generate a physical stress response against each of them, real or imagined, valid or neurotic. More than ever, we need to be smart and strategic about how we work with stress. We've already discussed three big lifestyle strategies: sleeping well, eating healthful food, and exercising regularly. Now we need to add friends, optimism, and spiritual practices, such as meditation and prayer.

The Friendship Factor

Caring friendship helps buffer bad news. Friends keep us from becoming isolated, a condition associated with sickness, discomfort, and general ineffectiveness. Friends also help us feel hopeful, a state of mind linked with higher levels of immune-system functioning. Good relationships remind us that there is something more important than whatever is currently causing our unhappiness.

According to a recent study conducted at UCLA, women are at an advantage when it comes to the friendship factor. A woman's biochemical response to stress is to connect with other people. Investigator Shelley E. Taylor, Ph.D., says that this "tend and befriend" response might be prompted by chemical messengers such as oxytocin that pour through a woman's body when she is stressed out. As she nurtures (tends) and protects (befriends) her children and others in her life, her physical state of hyperarousal settles down.[10]

Sadly, men don't enjoy the benefits of oxytocin

because testosterone counteracts its effects. But men can still derive a substantial stress-reduction benefit from the friendship factor. Laura Cousin Klein, Ph.D., assistant professor of Biobehavioral Health at Penn State University, worked with Taylor on this landmark study of women's stress response. Dr. Klein explains that many studies have shown that social ties reduce the risk of disease by lowering blood pressure, heart rate, and cholesterol levels. In one study, for example, researchers found that people who had no friends increased their risk of early death. In another study, those who had the most friends over time cut their risk of early death by more than 60 percent. The famed Harvard Nurses' Health Study (www.channing.harvard.edu/nhs/) from Harvard Medical School found that having more friends translates into a lowered likelihood of developing age-related physical impairments. In fact, the study concluded that not having close friends or confidants was as detrimental to health as obesity or smoking.

So how do we create social support to help us deal with stress? The demise of the small-town community and the fragmentation of the nuclear family have isolated us. Technology has reduced the need for face-to-face communications. Workaholism keeps us from enjoying leisure time and developing relationships that extend beyond the workday. Our focus on individual competence and self-reliance makes us uncomfortable — even embarrassed — to ask for help. It's clear that we need a few reminders to get us started:

- Don't expect one friend to cover all your emotional bases; it puts too much stress on the relationship. Cultivate several friends who support different aspects of you: a workout partner, an office compatriot, a hobby buddy, a spiritual companion.

- Accept assistance graciously. Don't feel guilty. Many helpers have experienced the same things as you. They can widen your perspective.

- Don't accept more help than you can tolerate. Your friends can do as much or as little as you want them to do.

- Give what you most want to get. Welcome opportunities to repay favors.

- Plan ahead. If you already know that a challenging time is on the way, such as surgery, a job status change, or a new baby in the family, start developing your support network now.

- If you feel awkward, concentrate your efforts on one person at a time. Ask for a simple favor. Practice.

Spiritual Practice

During the last 100 years, Western culture has done its best to be scientific and intellectual. We have devalued the soft, subjective stuff such as the spiritual and the transcendental. Hard science defines our reality. But things are changing.

A Positive Attitude

Optimism and a positive attitude are hardly considered spiritual states of mind, but they're often coupled with a religious calling or belief system. People with strong religious ties have a sense of purpose in life and they tend to frame events as being more than happenstance. They believe that their actions have a positive impact, no matter how their external circumstances appear. Far from devaluing their spiritual beliefs, stressful events often inspire a deeper call to action. The ability to find positive meaning in adversity may be one reason why actively religious people cope relatively well with crises, and why they describe themselves as happy more often than do nonreligious people.

Optimism is worth cultivating even if you're not the religious type. According to Barbara Fredrickson, a research psychologist at the University of Michigan, positive emotions, no matter what their source, have positive spin-offs. They "optimize health, subjective well-being, and psychological resilience." She suggests that positive states of mind can be encouraged or induced through relaxation techniques, such as meditation, invoking empathy and interest in a broader perspective.[11]

Manipulating facial muscles or posture can also improve one's disposition. For example, according to facial feedback studies by research psychologist Paul Eckman Ph.D., a hearty, raised-cheek smile generated by holding a pen between one's teeth can make cartoons seem funnier.[12] Researcher Sara Snodgrass studied the effects of walking behavior on mood. She found that taking long strides with arms swinging and eyes straight ahead made people feel happier than taking short, shuffling steps with eyes downcast.[13]

The nineteenth-century Polish poet Cyprian Norwid summed up the situation aptly:

To be what is called happy, one should have (1) something to live on, (2) something to live for, (3) something to die for. The lack of one of these results in drama. The lack of two results in tragedy.

Meditation

In the United States, almost 20 percent of the population meditates. According to Dharma Singh Khalsa, M.D., author of the book *Meditation As Medicine*, hundreds of studies have been conducted on the results of meditation. The conclusions are exciting:

- Meditation creates a unique hypometabolic state that lowers metabolism even more than sleep. As a result, oxygen consumption can drop by 10 to 20 percent.

- Meditation reduces blood lactate, which is a marker of stress and anxiety.

- Meditation increases production of the calming hormones melatonin and serotonin; it decreases levels of cortisol, the stress hormone.

- Meditation improves hearing, lowers blood pressure, and improves vision at close range.

- Long-term meditators experience 80 percent less heart disease and 50 percent less cancer than nonmeditators.

- Meditators secrete more of the youth-related hormone DHEA than nonmeditators. DHEA decreases stress, improves memory, preserves sexual function, and helps manage weight.

- After meditating, 75 percent of insomniacs sleep normally. (Sleeplessness is a classic symptom of too much stress.)

- After establishing a meditation practice, 34 percent of people suffering from chronic pain required significantly less medication. Chronic physical pain is exhausting and contributes significantly to keeping the body in a stressed-out, edgy condition.[14]

There are many styles of meditation practice, some with stronger connections to a particular religious faith. In my book *Meditation for Busy People*, I advocate *vipassana* (insight) meditation — a simple, nondenominational technique that focuses attention on the movement of the breath. As you gently and repeatedly bring your attention back to your breathing, insights can arise about your behavior, thought patterns, and emotions. Because Vipassana is a simple breathing technique, you can practice it whether you're sitting on a pillow, walking in a park, or standing in a grocery line.

Dr. Khalsa champions a powerful practice he calls "medical meditation." It targets specific health issues and combines yoga postures with controlled breath work, chanting, hand positions *(mudras)*, and mental focus. Medical meditation is a form of prescribed *kundalini* yoga, a practice that targets energy centers in the body (chakras), along with the endocrine system. The results are exciting, and Dr. Khalsa cites extensive research to supports its efficacy.

There are many other approaches to meditation: Transcendental, Zen, Tibetan, movement practices such as tai chi, and so on. With a little exploration, you can find a technique that suits your lifestyle and belief system. I describe my method on page 115.

While a regular meditation practice produces a wealth of positive results in your mind and body, perhaps the most important and least quantifiable result is the way it feeds your spiritual nature. Meditation connects you with your foundation as a living being, carrying your spiritual beliefs from intellectual concepts into heartfelt understanding. It fills the divine cup from which your spirit drinks. Whatever your definition of God, it can be felt and nourished in meditation.

Prayer

Religious practice has a definite positive correlation with health and longevity, rivaling the benefits of exercise and not smoking. Clinics and hospitals have historically been in close alliance with centers of religion; often the healer was also a spiritual leader. Today, the medical community maintains a careful distance from all things spiritual. Antibiotics and vaccinations have replaced prayer.

Larry Dossey, M.D., author of several books about prayer and medicine, has made it his life mission to welcome spiritual practice — specifically prayer — back into the medical community. Before his book *Healing Words* was published in 1993, only three U.S. medical schools offered courses that explored the role of religious practice and prayer in health; currently nearly eighty medical schools offer such courses.

Dr. Dossey's research clearly establishes the fact that prayer heals and helps; other sources confirm his conclusions. More than a dozen studies carried out at Duke University in Durham, North Carolina, show that religious activities such as praying improve health in a variety of ways, from maintaining lower blood pressure to boosting immune function and speeding recovery from depression.[15] Moreover, studies strongly suggest that the positive effects of prayer are not confined to a specific religion. All techniques of prayer appear to work equally well. However, a nondirective, "thy will be done" approach seems to set the stage for a greater effect than a directive style of prayer that specifies a particular outcome. It is also important that the person praying actually believes the prayer will produce positive results.

In an interview for *Bottom Line/Health*, Dr. Dossey said:

> If you believe prayer is a sham, it's unlikely you'll muster the requisite feelings that seem to make prayer work. The same principle applies when praying for yourself (petitionary prayer). You must first accept the efficacy of prayer — regardless of whether you think it works because of a supreme being or simply as a result of caring and empathy.[16]

Dr. Dossey also emphasizes love as a critical component. Double-blind studies showed that the effectiveness of prayer for someone else (intercessionary prayer) was positively influenced by empathy, love, and compassion.

Medical files are filled with miracles that appear to result from prayer; we are now seeing the value of prayer validated scientifically. (Some people find this particularly amusing: using science to validate God.) There are many explanations of how prayer functions, but it really doesn't matter. The bottom line is that prayer is a good practice to include in your list of stress-management strategies because it works.

▲▲▲

If, after reading this chapter, you still feel paralyzed by the drama in your life, let me offer a final word. No matter how pressing your current issues may seem, they typically have a short, intense shelf life. Tomorrow, next month, next year you'll hardly remember what drove you to distraction today. However, these same issues can leave a legacy of weakened bones, extra body weight, neuromuscular degeneration, relationship problems, and immune-system damage that can cascade and multiply. If there was ever a time to get serious about stress reduction, it is now.

3

....

living in a
complicated world

The complexities of life are at once disturbing and compelling. No one wants pollution, yet we depend on petroleum-based products such as makeup, tires, and medicinal salves. No one wants rampant deforestation, yet many of us live and work in wood-framed buildings, walk on wooden floors, and recline in wooden furniture. The natural world cannot continue to be consumed at the current rate, yet Western society — representing about 6 percent of the world's population — uses a whopping 55 percent of its resources. And lastly, everyone craves harmony and balance in their lives, yet our society glorifies the achievements of workaholics. We've lost the sense that life is profound and purposeful — that it's much more than buying, getting, and hoarding.

When I look at stress reduction in the context of our modern lifestyle, I feel like throwing up my hands in disgust and frustration. Pop culture creates insatiable cravings to be faster, stronger, younger, sexier. These cravings drive us to make unfulfilling choices that have no lasting value, keeping us restless and apprehensive. But, as I've often said to friends, the fact that green lipstick is available doesn't mean I have to buy it. There are alternatives. In this chapter, I'll talk about slowing down enough — even in times of extreme pressure — to take advantage of alternatives that will empower us instead of driving us farther into complexity and anxiety.

What to Do in a Crisis

At this point, we've learned some specific ways to help our bodies become stress-hardy. We understand the importance of implementing these broadscale self-improvement strategies right away, and we know that they will make a big difference in the long run. But what do we do in the middle of a crisis? How can we marshal our energies so that we can respond intelligently and quickly instead of panicking and flipping out?

Let me share with you a simple system that I use to handle stress. It consists of three steps:

1. move your body,

2. narrow your focus, and

3. take action.

These steps are easy to remember, which is important when your brain goes into overload. But, even better, they are adaptable to almost any situation. Whether you're confronted with a big drama or the same old annoyances, these three simple steps can help you respond in ways that are wholesome and empowering.

Step 1: Move Your Body

When something happens to freak you out, the first thing you need to do is handle the surge of energy that's pushing through your system. As we discussed in chapter 1, this hormonal surge was designed to create quick action when you're about to be eaten by a tiger, and it hasn't changed biologically since the time when tigers were reasonable threats.

The problem you are currently facing likely isn't a tiger and won't be solved by running away as fast as you can. You'll be more successful using a less direct route: changing your mental state through the pathway of the physical. Because the body and mind are so closely connected, changing one does change the other. Indeed, many people believe they should be referenced as a single unit: bodymind.

Physical movement can alter your state of mind with surprising ease. When you walk, run, or even swim, your body takes up most of your energy and expels it through repeated muscular contractions. You are literally pushing the anxiety out through your arms and legs.

Try an experiment: Walk briskly for five minutes or more while paying attention to your body. Feel the energy settle into a rhythmic pattern. Even five minutes of fast walking and deep breathing can make room for an emotional shift. What you're really looking to do is shift your overwhelmed mental state into a less acute, more thoughtful mode. There may not be an immediate solution to your problem, but you will be ready to recognize one when it presents itself. Luck favors the prepared. Furthermore, the mental change has physical longevity because it is supported by neurochemicals released via the exercise.

The easiest form of movement is to simply go for a walk. Include periodic deep abdominal breathing to expand your tightened chest. Walk around the block. Walk around the building. Even pacing back and forth can be useful; say to yourself "lifting, moving, placing" as you lift, move, and place each foot into the next step. If you're walking fast, try saying "step, step, step." When your mind wanders back into anxiety, return it gently to your footfall. This transforms walking into a form of meditation. After fifteen minutes of walking meditation, your mind should have enough space to entertain possibilities instead of just problems.

There are other forms of physical exercise that you can do instead of walking: yoga, tai chi, weight training. The only problem is that slow, deliberate movement can be a challenge when stress is skyrocketing. If you're too wound up, a quick walk will soothe you in preparation for slower practices.

While you move, you may want to recite (or chant) a mantra — an empowering phrase or sound combination that, when repeated, helps clear your head and center your energy. In Sanskrit, the word "mantra" has two parts: "man," which means "mind," and "tra," which means "deliverance." Mantras can be chanted in English — for example, "Peace fills my heart," "I am one with God," or "Thy will be done." Mantras may also use words and tones from other languages, such as the Buddhist mantra "Om Mani Padme Hum," or a common mantra used in kundalini yoga, "Sa Ta Na Ma." Acting as a form of positive self-talk, a mantra helps open your mind, creating space for new ideas or the upwelling of peace. The mantra is not meant to deny your suffering, and if it is primarily tonal in nature (not words) it may not even make intellectual sense. However, the more you use the mantra, the more you invest it with your energy. It gives your anxiety something to chew on, leaving other parts of your mind free to problem-solve or simply rest.

Step 2: Narrow Your Focus

At this point, it is easy to drop into overwhelming worry. Despite your walking, you still have a big problem to contend with. Slow abdominal breathing can help you keep a clear head. It reverses the stress response. It helps you concentrate. Gently expand and contract your belly, breathing deeply and easily through your nose if possible.

Begin to consider what you can do just this week, just today, just this hour. How small do you need to make the time frame in order to feel positive? Don't worry about details; just focus on one baby step. What can you do in the next five minutes?

Sometimes a physical movement or sensation can break an emotional tailspin. Decide in advance what you're going to do and connect it with a positive behavior or mantra. You could click your fingers, clap your hands together, or wear a rubber band around your wrist and snap it whenever you start to plummet emotionally. It reminds you to handle the moment and little else. The first few times aren't easy; when the mind gets into a tailspin, it has momentum. But with practice, these little tricks will help you come back to center.

When my mother had a stroke, I was in the middle of handling a thousand responsibilities. These things never happen at convenient times. I couldn't stop living, my children needed me, and I was busy with work. No matter where I was, I needed to be somewhere else. Even though I have a cadre of supportive friends, there are some things you just have to do yourself. Every time I went to the hospital or the nursing home, I became overwhelmed by emotional and physical demands. I knew that the only way I was going to manage living with a semblance of sanity was by taking one thing at a time and doing what was in front of me first. So I narrowed my focus by literally looking at my feet. Whenever I felt that surge of "Oh my God...," I'd look down at my feet and tap them on the ground. My mantra was, "The next half hour, the next half hour." I discovered that I could get a lot done by living my life in half-hour increments.

Panic is short-lived if you don't give it energy. It feels urgent and irresistible, but it quickly transforms into plain old garden-variety anxiety as your attention is redirected and narrowed. You can work with anxiety; it's panic that immobilizes you. In my case, I learned to play the game of doing what I could for the next half hour, and by the end of the day I actually felt better. It might not have been elegant, but I handled what needed to be done. I built on my successes, no matter how small. Day by day, I moved through the crises with a growing sense of self-confidence.

When you narrow your focus, you shut out distractions and become centered in the here and now. In the midst of crisis, you're actually maneuvering through a spiritual space because you are riveted in the moment. Amazing as it sounds, this is an exhilarating experience — which is why so many people are addicted to drama. But the goal isn't to create a crisis so that we can live in the moment. We shouldn't eschew daily life in search of the perfect galvanizing extreme. Rather, our goal should be to learn how to live in the moment so that all experiences, no matter how mundane, can nourish, energize, and enthrall us. Life shouldn't be about crisis; it should be about joy.

Step 3: Take Action

Feeling powerless is a big contributor to stress, and the remedy is action, doing something. Many people take destructive action, such as eating too much or drinking their stress away. That's not what I'm talking about. I'm referring to wholesome, life-affirming action. Your two preparatory steps — moving your body and narrowing your focus — have readied you for this.

The action you take doesn't have to be dramatic to be empowering. It may not even be directly related to the problem at hand. Anything positive helps. Action creates momentum. Taking a small, positive step toward handling the crisis can be enormously liberating. For example, if you're steeped in debt, the act of paying off one small bill or paying back a friend — or even of shopping and deciding *not* to buy something (breaking a pattern of behavior) — can make you feel that there's a way out.

Some people wash windows or floors when they become upset. They are moving their bodies, narrowing their focus, and taking action all with the same activity. They may not be able to describe precisely why cleaning helps them manage their stress or solve their problems; they only know that it works. So do something positive — anything, no matter how small.

Television and movies give us a picture of how disaster should be handled: with a smirk and a fast kick. If you go numb, break down crying, or scream, you may feel like a failure. But, let me remind you of something: fictional characters live at their peak all the time. We can't live that way. Big-screen heroes and supermodels set a flawless standard of perennial youth and beauty. We aren't airbrushed that way. The characters in movies and on television have been rewritten and rehearsed so often that every expression and nuance is polished to a sheen. We aren't scripted that way.

Don't use the technique of taking action as another opportunity to bludgeon yourself with disappointment. If you can't quite get it together to do something useful, go back to Steps One and Two. Do them again. Never blame yourself for an honest, unskillful response to a crisis. If you feel powerless, angry, trapped, or terrified, that's okay; it's human.

Living in an Age of Fear

Our world can be a scary place. It has always been scary, but with more people, dwindling resources, and better coverage of the world's suffering, it feels — and indeed is — even scarier now. The big question is how can we be smart about the risks of living, without becoming overwhelmed with paranoia? The answer is to practice the three empowering steps described above: move your body, narrow your focus, take action. Instead of pretending that your anxiety has no basis (which is almost impossible, given the news we're subjected to), face it directly and practice handling it.

> "What ought one to say, then, as each hardship comes? I was practicing for this, I was training for this."
>
> — Epictetus

Think about weight lifting for a minute. You lift weights to develop strength and endurance, but you don't start with a 50-pound weight. Instead, you begin by lifting 5 and 10 pounds until you build up the strength to lift more. Use the same strategy in your stress-management training. You're working to develop tolerance and grace under pressure. Decide today that when something stressful comes up, no matter how small, you will practice the three empowering steps.

Consider the stories of John and Sarah, two people who faced their fears and restored their sense of capability under stress.

John

John was a computer programmer whose well-deserved week of vacation was in jeopardy. New product developments forced him to rewrite a program that was set to ship in just twenty-four hours — the first day of John's holiday. He'd made travel plans, but if his material wasn't ready, he couldn't leave and the product couldn't ship. Already exhausted from a tiring work schedule, he sat in front of his computer, paralyzed and enraged. The longer he sat, the more upset he became and the less he could accomplish.

John knew he had to break the cycle of anxiety that was controlling him. He started by taking several slow, deep breaths, paying attention to his body and not his whirling mental state. Next, he decided to go for a long walk. The act of walking was a conscious decision over which he had ultimate authority. It felt good to take a little control. Walking flushed the anxiety through his limbs and gave his mind a brief rest.

When he returned to his desk, John was surprised at how refreshed he felt. His mind was sharpened. As he began to take action by typing, his fear arose again. He felt stymied, but his mind remained clear from the walking and the fresh air. After a few minutes, he decided that he was trying to do too much. So he narrowed his focus and set a small goal that could be accomplished within a half hour. He did the same thing for the second half hour and the third, each small accomplishment building on the others. He told himself that he could only accomplish what was humanly possible, trying not to add perfectionism to the pressure he already felt. John allowed himself to take walking breaks and a short night of sleep, always returning to the task with a clear intention. John completed his project and, tired but successful, started his vacation a day late. He rearranged his travel plans and negotiated a couple of extra days at the end of his holiday as comp time.

Sarah

At a routine medical visit, Sarah was diagnosed with a stage-three aggressive cancer. She was raising two young children, maintaining a busy career as a teacher, and receiving child support from her ex-husband.

Reeling from the diagnosis, her emotional state

swung back and forth between numbness and rage. Nighttime was the worst. She'd wake up at 2:00 A.M., her body shivering with fear. How would she cope with this terrible situation? How could she take care of her children? What about radiation or chemotherapy? What about the cost? These stress attacks were exhausting and debilitating, chipping away at the sleep she so desperately needed.

One night, instead of anxiously pacing and shivering, she did something deliberate: she did yoga. The process of taking action instead of reacting (which is often the source of pacing) gave her enough emotional space to narrow her field of vision. Instead of looking at the big picture of cancer, she looked to the end of the week. What needed to be done by Friday? Because she still felt overwhelmed, she backed up to looking at the next day. What did she need to do to get through tomorrow — something she could handle without increasing the panic? It was still too much. Was there one small thing she could do right then to help get her life back?

She stood up from her stretching and cleaned and reorganized her purse. It seemed simple, but her purse was her nerve center and it had become as overwhelmed with trash as her mind. After her purse was ready and parked by the door, she began to yawn, went back to bed, and fell asleep quickly. The next morning she had one less thing to do, and that small action gave her encouragement.

Sarah continued to follow her regimen whenever she awoke with a stress attack. The simple steps of moving her body, narrowing her focus, and taking small actions rebuilt her sense of power and control. She was better able to assess her family's needs and ask for help.

Sarah reevaluated her life and made changes in her dietary and exercise habits. She took action when she could, and stopped obsessing over circumstances she couldn't change. She took a leave of absence from work, developed a robust meditation practice as she battled the cancer, and enlisted her children in helping with household tasks. Today Sarah is free of cancer, and she volunteers to help others in similar circumstances.

Fear Is Not Always the Truth

Fear is fueled by imagination. Imagination can construct scary things that aren't real and draw false conclusions. The problem is that most of us don't know how to argue with it; we tend to believe the stories that fear tells us. As a result, we live defensively, in ignorance and constant agitation. This is no way to be happy.

Fear must be questioned. What is its source? This root cause is full of information. Typically, the thing we fear isn't as overwhelming as the story it presents. You must separate the story from the reality to make skillful, high-road decisions about what to do next. Do you have all the facts? Are you willing to step back from habitual emotional reactivity and do something that won't feed the alienation and anxiety? This is where the three empowering steps discussed above can make a difference.

I have a dear friend whose job is to step around fear. She identifies and arranges treatment for adolescent sex offenders. As a parent of young children, I recoil at the thought of such a responsibility. One day over tea, I asked her, "How can you be effective with young sex offenders? You have a daughter to protect; don't these kids scare the bejesus out of you?"

"Sure they scare me sometimes," she answered carefully. "But I can't let fear take over. These kids are wounded and angry. If I can uncover their wounds, I can begin to see what might help them. They're still young and their patterns of behavior can change. So even though I feel afraid, I also feel hopeful."

My friend knows how to step back from fear and get the facts. She looks beyond a heinous act and finds the simple humanity underneath it. Fear doesn't paralyze her. As such, she is able to deliver a critical service to her clients — and certainly to the rest of us as a society.

Fear isn't without purpose. It is useful when it prompts smart action, such as avoiding train tracks and dark alleys. But because fear is such a compelling, primitive state of mind, it can quickly overwhelm us. When it takes control, we think, "I am afraid." This may feel accurate, but it is exaggerated and incorrect. A more skillful, precise assessment would be, "There is fear in me." Fear is triggered by all kinds of imaginary stimuli. It comes and goes. When you correctly identify it as an emotional weather pattern blowing through your mind ("Oh, there it goes!"), you can see around and through it. You are not fear itself; you are bigger than that.

Children and Stress

Like adults, all children experience anxiety, especially during specific stages of development. Young children

....

may experience short-lived fears, such as fear of the dark. They also show intense distress at being separated from Mom or Dad throughout the preschool years. Older children and teens can periodically become frustrated with classroom expectations or by squabbles with family members and friends. Anxiety is a natural response to painful, frustrating situations, and we all learn how to cope with a certain amount of life's insecurities.

However, kids today are under increasing stress, no matter where they live or what kind of family they live with. Many lead hectic lives that rival those of their busy parents. From schoolwork to music lessons to after-school sports, these children suffer from time pressure, pressure to perform, pressure to get good grades, and peer pressure. Even the physical changes associated with puberty appear to be starting at an earlier age. It can take a toll on a child's health, happiness, and school performance.

Parents must be alert, because signs of too much stress are not always overt. For example, anxious children are often overly tense or uptight. Their worries may prevent healthy participation in school or after-school activities.

If a child shows what appears to be unreasonable

discomfort or anxiety, try discussing it in a neutral, non-threatening manner. Never discount the child's fears. The problem could be a natural age-appropriate concern, it could be stress-related, or it could be something concrete that demands action. If necessary, consult a therapist who specializes in working with children.

Here are just a few of the many stresses with which our children must cope:

- Too many activities
- Not enough relaxation time
- High expectations
- Busy, distracted, or ailing parents
- Political and world problems
- Lack of extended family support
- Parental or peer pressure
- Low family income
- Poor nutrition
- Bodily changes
- Negative thoughts and feelings about themselves
- School demands and frustrations

- An unsafe living environment or neighborhood
- Moving or changing schools

The effects of ongoing, excessive stress can be devastating to a child's health and well-being, leading to a wide range of problems, including:

- Trouble with sleep
- Irritability, grouchiness
- Anger, frustration, possible violence
- Alienation, possible gang involvement
- Depression, suicide, running away from home
- Addictions: cigarettes, drugs, alcohol
- Teenage pregnancy
- Poor performance in school, dropping out of school
- Frequent illness, poor digestion, upset stomach
- Lack of self-confidence

As with adults, children need resources to help them manage the anxiety that comes from living in the modern world. But because children can't do it themselves, you as the responsible adult or parent must provide resources for them. Here are a few suggestions to help you get started:

- *Educate your children about stress.* Describe what happens to the body and why they feel so antsy. Tell them that physical changes happen whenever a situation is perceived as difficult or painful. Explain that these changes help us respond to danger, and that as soon as we decide that the situation isn't so dangerous, our bodies calm down.

- *Model stress-management skills.* Let your children see how you include stress-management in your repertoire of personal behavior. When you're getting upset, say out loud, "Look how upset I'm getting. I'm breathing fast and feeling very nervous. I'm going to stop for a moment and take a couple of slow, deep breaths before I do anything else." Children who learn stress-management skills feel less helpless and have more choices when responding to stressors.

- *Make sure children exercise and eat regularly.* If their bodies aren't healthy, it's much more challenging for children to cope with stress.

- *Avoid excess caffeine intake by way of coffee drinks or soda pop.* Caffeine increases feelings of anxiety and agitation. Many drinks marketed to children contain caffeine, so be sure to read labels.

- *Teach children simple relaxation techniques.* Most kids, just like most adults, don't know how to focus on abdominal breathing or how to consciously relax their muscles. Consider taking a "yoga for kids" class with your child. Guide your child into a deep body relaxation as a prelude to sleep.

- *Teach children to express their anxieties using words instead of aggressive actions.* Ask them to use "I feel…" sentences to help them identify and communicate their feelings, such as "I feel sad when you ignore me."

- *Talk about the value of rehearsal.* If a child is afraid of attending a birthday party, suggest rehearsing strategies for handling it. The child can take a couple of deep, slow breaths, then pretend to walk into the party, heading for the punch bowl.

- *Teach children how to divide big projects into little, achievable tasks.* This will engender practical coping skills that can serve them in the classroom as well as when they become part of the workforce.

- *Decrease negative self-talk.* Talk to children about how energy follows thought. If they tell themselves they're bad or stupid, they're more likely to fulfill that prophecy. Teach them to challenge negative thoughts with neutral or positive thoughts. "I'll never have friends" can be transformed into "I may feel alone now, but I will make friends if I work at it."

- *Try not to feed unrealistic expectations.* If a child is a perfectionist, reinforce being "good enough" instead of flawless.

- *Exemplify and teach the value of taking breaks to listen to music, walk, or visit with friends.* These breaks don't necessarily include passively watching television because television isn't restful and typically doesn't stimulate creative thinking.

- *Encourage children to share their burdens with you.* Children need to talk about their problems so they can strategize ways to handle them, and also to clear their minds and be heard. Talk with them. Offer them opportunities to share. Keep in mind that they may attempt to protect you from their concerns if they sense that you are under stress yourself. You may need to reassure them that your problems are being handled and that you have plenty of emotional room to listen.

- *Take time to talk with your children early on in their development.* As your child approaches the pressure cooker of middle school and high school, it is critical to have avenues for communication defined and well practiced. Start talking with them while they are young; don't put it off.

- *Encourage children to develop allies.* Kids need friends they can trust and who understand

them. Talk to them about creating a network of friends to help them manage aca-
demic and social pressures.

- *Guide children into practices of giving and charity.*
Help them appreciate how good it feels to
share their bounty. Nothing relieves a feeling of victimization better than doing
something good for someone else.

Helping Children Cope with Global Crisis

The tragedy of the World Trade Center's destruc-
tion on September 11, 2001, brought home to Americans
what many other families in war-torn countries have
been dealing with for years: the devastating impact of
terrorism and war, and their effect on children. These
traumas can provoke ongoing difficulties and a form of
extreme stress known as "post-traumatic stress disorder"
(PTSD). According to the American Academy of Child
and Adolescent Psychiatry (www.aacap.org), a child's
risk of developing PTSD is related to:

1. the seriousness of the trauma,

2. whether the trauma is repeated,

3. the child's proximity to the trauma, and

4. the child's relationship to the victim(s).

Children with PTSD may:

- have frequent memories of the event — or, in young children, engage in play that repeatedly reenacts the trauma;

- experience upsetting and frightening dreams;

- act or feel like the experience is happening again;

- develop repeated physical or emotional symptoms when the child is reminded of the event;

- worry about dying at an early age;

- lose interest in activities;

- become emotionally numb and withdrawn or depressed;

- act out rage, despair, horror, or denial;

- act younger than their age (for example, clingy or whiny behavior, thumb-sucking);

- have problems concentrating, sleeping, or handling emotions.

These responses aren't abnormal in the context of the catastrophic events. However, when they continue indefinitely or seem to get worse, it's time to consult a therapist or child psychologist who specializes in PTSD. Early intervention is critical.

What can you do to help a child handle serious disaster, such as the devastation witnessed on 9/11?

- *Acknowledge the danger, but reinforce safety.* Falsely minimizing the threat will not end a child's concerns. Instead, try to acknowledge the frightening aspects of the situation and then reinforce and nurture a feeling of safety. For example, "Yes, the war is really scary, but Mom and Dad are doing everything possible to keep you safe. Our home is secure, and all our friends are helping us."

- *Distance the child from the threat.* Children can feel personally targeted and in danger, even if a threat is random and unlikely to occur

again. You need to create a sense of distance from it. For example, "Even though
you've seen it on TV, you're actually very far
away from it."

- *Keep up your routine.* Aside from unavoidable
upsets, attempt to keep the day-to-day routine of the household stable and predictable.
Young children are especially grounded and
reassured by routine.

▲▲▲

Real life isn't smooth, predictable, or timely. It is cha-
otic, sometimes dangerous, and frequently exhilarating.
There are many ways to successfully navigate the rough
spots, most of them messy; in the real world, things
don't have to be pretty. If you make it through a stressful situation without dying or killing someone — hey,
you did okay.

We can't change the times in which we live; these
are the circumstances we and our children were born
to handle. But we do have a choice: we can either drown
ourselves in familiar, unhealthy, denial-based habits, or

we can flex our muscles and take three steps toward positive change: move our bodies, narrow our focus, and take action. These steps empower us no matter what kind of wave knocks us over. When we're proactive, we're not drowning; we're swimming.

4

....

spiritual goal-setting

Modern life can be deeply stressful and confusing because of its complexity. Like a maze with too many directions, life fosters anxiety because it is difficult to know which way to go. This chapter can help you navigate the labyrinth by embracing two big "G" words: Goals and God.

Goals help you define your direction, gather your energy, and cut through a dizzying amount of distraction. They relieve stress because they provide a conduit for wholesome, positive action.

Inaction fuels helplessness, generating the worst kinds of stressful states of mind: desperation and despondency. We become trapped in habit patterns of negative thinking, blind to opportunities, victimized by powerlessness. Setting goals helps reverse these conditions. By defining targets and taking small, consistent steps toward them, we clear a path through the complexity. Instead of being stuck, we become empowered.

Of course there is much more to life than setting and achieving goals. Life can be shallow and self-centered if it lacks an expansive connection to the infinite creative presence known as God (Goddess, Brahma, Buddha nature, Christ consciousness, Allah, Life, Being, Spirit). When we unite ourselves with a loving, inclusive God, we are lit from within. We no longer feel driven to define ourselves by approval or results. We build a consciousness that can move with equanimity through frustration, fear, and pain. We are naturally inclined to walk what Colleen and Bob MacGilchrist (authors of *Match! Simple Strategies for Happily Ever After*) describe as "the high road." High-road decisions are skillful and loving. They reduce stress and minimize conflict because they are responsive, respectful, and collaborative. The MacGilchrists say, "Taking the high road creates a peaceful spaciousness that allows the grace of God to reopen your heart.... Conflict can evolve into something easier to manage, or it can go away entirely."

What Is Spiritual Goal-Setting?

When goals become partnered with awakening to God, it yields a process I call "spiritual goal-setting." Spiritual goal-setting is a tool for much more than simple acquisition of things and management of life's confusion. When goal-setting is spiritualized, results are not the main focus; it is the process we care about. Through the process, we grow, learn, and awaken. The goal itself is merely icing on the cake.

Spiritual goal-setting works in partnership with desire — a tricky combination. Desire creates energy, but it must be steadied with equanimity, compassion, and a growing sense of being spiritually complete exactly as you are. Otherwise, it spins you in circles, treading over the same tired ground, generating an inexhaustible drive for more.

The ultimate purpose of spiritual goal-setting is to explore and strengthen qualities of being that bring enduring happiness: loving-kindness, courage, composure, tenacity, generosity, compassion, insight, and humor. These qualities are beyond the limited world of desire and acquisition. When we operate from a center of divinity that embraces these qualities, we no longer experience stress; we experience liberation.

There are a few foundation principles upon which spiritual goal-setting rests:

- *You are not your thoughts.* Your thoughts don't define you. They are like clouds in the sky. They are generated by any number of stimuli, many of which are grounded in memory and fantasy. You are much bigger than your thoughts. The less you identify with them, the more freedom you'll feel and the more insight you'll experience. When an unwelcome thought grabs your attention, you can say, "Oh look, there's that thought again. Isn't that interesting?" Meditation practice is an excellent way to develop this skill.

- *You are never alone.* Loneliness often seems to walk hand in hand with spiritual awakening. As we expand into our relationship with God, we shed our limiting beliefs and narrow definitions of who we are. This is why it is so important to begin each day with a spiritual practice such as meditation or prayer. You step back from your loneliness, seeing the greater picture and the greater you. In the silence, there is comfort and warm support from the universe. And you will probably attract new friends and companions who will keep you company along the path.

- *Small steps lead to big triumphs.* When working on an important project, people tend to want fast, dramatic results. They devalue small steps, searching for shortcuts and easy answers. Then they wonder why they fail. They forget that every successful path is walked step-by-step. Each step is difficult or impossible to take without having taken the previous step. The more challenging the proj-ect, the smaller the steps may need to be. Marathon runner and author Tawni Gomes trumpets "baby steps" as her primary strategy for changing a lifetime of unhealthy habits; that is how she stepped out of a wheelchair, dropped 100 pounds, and evolved into an athlete and a nationally recognized motivational leader (www.connectingconnectors.com).

"Look at a stonecutter hammering away at his rock, perhaps a hundred times without as much as a crack showing in it. Yet at the hundred-and-first blow it will split in two, and I know it was not the last blow that did it, but all that had gone before."

— Jacob A. Riis, journalist and social reformer

- *Fear comes with the territory.* Stop thinking that fear must vanish before you can start a project. Fear is part of life. You hear it when you're perched on your growing edge. Tilt your head to listen, and then press on. Demystify the fear by saying, "There's the same old fear sitting on my shoulder. I'll just go about my business." You'll know in your heart if it is appropriate or paranoid. Attending to fear without losing your emotional balance is a simple, powerful skill that develops quickly with practice.

- *Every day is a new beginning.* Zen Master Shunryu Suzuki Roshi says, "In the beginner's mind are infinite possibilities, in the expert's mind very few."[17] A beginner's mind allows for a new view of an old situation. It is especially helpful when you feel like you're off target, when you've made mistakes, or when old, unskillful habits reassert themselves. Through the eyes of a beginner, you can see each day as a new opportunity to wipe the slate clean. It doesn't matter what happened yesterday; today you start fresh with no mistakes. Quoting scholar Edward Said, "Beginning is not only a kind of action, it is also a frame of mind, a kind of work, an attitude, a consciousness."[18]

How to Set Spiritual Goals

The Buddha talked about the importance of cultivating four states of mind: equanimity, loving-kindness, compassion, and joy in others' successes — states collectively known as the "heavenly abodes." The more they arise, the more happiness we experience. Stress has no room to take root.

Spiritual goal-setting provides a wonderful opportunity for cultivating the heavenly abodes. How? The answer is simple: through generosity. The driving energy behind spiritual goal-setting is generosity. As you'll read below, every goal is extended into a generous action. The Buddha says that, in a single act of generosity, all four heavenly abodes are experienced equally.

> "We make a living by what we get; we make a life by what we give."
>
> — Sir Winston Churchill

Now to the specifics. The process of spiritual goal-setting can be divided into three parts:

1. Declare your goal;
2. Define your extension;
3. Design your process.

Declare Your Goal

Goals must be measurable. Make your goal as specific as possible so that you'll know when it is achieved. It should also have an end date or condition. On her website (www.chellie.com), educator and businesswoman Chellie Campbell, author of *The Wealthy Spirit: Daily Affirmations for Financial Stress Reduction*, defines a goal as a dream with a deadline. Here are a few simple examples:

- Submit my book manuscript to publishers until a contract is offered and accepted.

- Finish my yearly status report at the office by the end of this month.

- Ride my first century (100-mile) bike ride by September 1 of next year.

- Reorganize the garage (floor cleaned, tools stored, workbench built, excess donated) by Labor Day.

- Practice at least twenty minutes of daily meditation for the next thirty days.

Define Your Extension

This is where you extend your goal into an act of generosity. Some goals are naturally noble; others need to be expanded a bit. Find a way to serve others with the goal you have set for yourself. Here are a few examples:

- Once I receive my book contract, I'll donate at least 10 percent of my advance to the local animal shelter.

- Once I finish my status report, I'll take my spouse out for a special dinner.

- After my first century bike ride, I'll contact my neighborhood association to organize a ride for the kids.

- After the garage is reorganized, I will host a "thanks for the help" party for my kids and their friends. I'll also surprise them with a special storage cubby for their book bags and coats.

- After one month of daily meditation, I'll volunteer a full day of service to my church in celebration of my commitment to practice.

By extending your goal into charitable action, you fuel your enthusiasm for achieving it. Each act of charity brings you happiness in three ways: the pleasure of the planning, the joy of actually doing it, and the warmth of the memory. Generosity is a delight and a relief. It is the ultimate stress reducer. Through generosity, the uptight, demanding energy we sometimes bring to our projects is either expelled or never really has a chance to develop.

My friend Bob complained about this step. "Why should I extend my goal into a generous action? I already put in a million work hours to support my family. My whole life is a generous action!"

Let me clarify: The idea is to include generosity as part of your goal; it doesn't have to be a staggering effort. Make the extension something you will enjoy or care about doing. For example, if Bob decides that he is going to submit his taxes on time this year, he could extend his goal into a special trip to the park with his children.

Like Bob, you may be burdened with "daily grind" responsibilities that feel emotionally and spiritually empty. You're probably careful not to squander what little energy you have left at the end of the day, but energy and happiness grow from sharing, not hoarding — from emptying your cup so that it may be filled again. This is accomplished by acts of conscious, openhanded generosity. It may be challenging to get started, but no lesson is more important to learn.

Design Your Process

This is where you divide the goal-setting process into bite-sized pieces. There are a thousand ways to do this, but my favorite is to reverse-engineer the project. I take the end product (the goal) and work backward using a calendar to schedule interim goals. Walking backward through time, I usually get a pretty solid list of tasks. I write them in pencil because I'll probably need to rework them as the process unfolds. I then look at the task closest to the present and divide it into smaller steps. Once I finish working with one task, I'll divide up the next task on the calendar. Sometimes reverse engineering isn't required. Every goal, every situation is a little different; you have to be flexible.

Naturally, you want to be able to check off your interim goals as you accomplish them, but busy people always live complicated lives. You'll probably need to reschedule and perhaps even renegotiate the end result. When you're stymied and you can't see around the corner, try taking even smaller steps. Big leaps can work, but they tend to be intuitive and serendipitous — an unexpected confluence of circumstance. It's a case of fortune favoring the prepared.

A final word about this process: always include quiet time for meditation or prayer. Try starting and ending your day with a spiritual practice. It will help transform a potentially self-centered effort into an openhearted, creative sharing of universal abundance.

Common Excuses for Not Setting Goals

When people don't set goals, they usually have good excuses. I'll discuss some of the most common excuses and offer a spiritual perspective on each.

I Can't Pick a Goal

Some lucky folks have only one aspiration weighing on their minds, making it easy to choose a goal. Others can't seem to focus on anything specific. They're either overwhelmed with possibilities or they're indecisive and nothing stands out. In either case, there are many ways to get around it. Try any of the following suggestions:

- Choose a goal that's easy to meet. Build your confidence by starting small.

- Work on organization first. That is, pick a goal that provides a foundation for your efforts: clearing your desk, organizing your files, updating your software, cleaning out

your closet. It's much easier to start an important project when your world is more orderly.

- Pick something that involves another person. Working as a team is a great way to
  keep up your motivation and energy.

- Divide goals into two groups: complicated
  and simple. Pick one from the "simple" side.

- Which goal do you instinctively turn away
  from? Perhaps tackling the most challenging
  goal first is the best way to wake up your
  energy.

- Write some goals on little pieces of paper
  and stick them to a dartboard, then throw a
  dart at them. Voilà! Your goal is selected!

- Try something off the wall. Take up aikido
  or decide to grow vegetables in your yard. A
  new project can be revitalizing and will generate energy for the other goals on your list.
  This is because energy and momentum
  empower you. Their positive effects are felt
  throughout your world, not just in one area.

- Have your best friend choose a goal for you.
  Often, friends can see things you can't.

Enlist your friend as a goal buddy to help define your direction and support you when you feel like giving up.

THE SPIRITUAL PERSPECTIVE: Relax. It doesn't matter which goal you choose. All actions foster awakening — the real purpose of your existence. If you're feeling particularly burdened by the decision process, ask for comfort and direction during prayer time. Then get started on something — anything — and listen for your guidance to come through action, not idleness.

I'm Not Motivated

Most people expect to ride motivation like they might surf a wave. They hang back, biding their time, assuming that the perfect curl will suddenly appear and carry them easily. They say things like: "I'll start that project when I feel motivated," "I'm just not ready, I guess," or "It's not the right time yet."

The problem is that motivation is unpredictable; it waxes and wanes with your circumstances and emotions. For example, if you sprain your back, fear can motivate you to take up yoga. If your check bounces, embarrassment can motivate you to balance your checkbook. Events are as unpredictable as the incentive they generate. Don't wait. Enthusiasm and motivation build up faster and more reliably when you take action first.

THE SPIRITUAL PERSPECTIVE: Emotional states are interesting, powerful, and compelling, but they should not be the only fuel you use to generate action. When you center yourself in Being, you become open to the infinite source of energy that never runs dry. That source doesn't rely on emotion or circumstances, and its foundation is generosity of spirit. From this vantage point, you take action because it is your divine nature to do so.

I Don't Follow Through

Think about how upset you would feel if your best friend told you that you were no longer trustworthy. You'd need to have a long honest talk, then make it a priority to follow through with your promises. Well, you also have a trust relationship with yourself. When self-trust is weak, you don't believe in your own ability to follow through with commitments. You resist meaningful projects. If you do try something big, your stress load will shoot way up and you won't be able to tolerate the burden. You'll give up.

Fortunately, trust in yourself is something you can rebuild. First, you must release the vision of yourself as untrustworthy. This is more difficult than it first appears because unreliability has a payoff: someone else does the hard stuff, and you get to take it easy. But doing hard stuff builds self-confidence and self-respect; it crafts your character. Hard projects are typically more interesting and satisfying to complete. If you don't take on hard stuff like maintaining relationships, staying healthy, or meeting career goals, you become boring and colorless. You never dance on your growing edge. You stagnate.

Second, you must forgive yourself for your past bad behavior. Continued blame and self-hatred will undermine your efforts. Guilt and blame don't change the past. The best way to make up for past wrongs is by making better choices. Remember, energy follows thought. If your dominant thinking remains self-destructive, it will be hard to change your behavior — and this is the kind of "hard" you'd be smart to avoid. Consider attempting a project that you feel reasonably sure you can complete successfully. Lost trust is like muscle tone; it can be regained, but you have to start small and build it up over time.

THE SPIRITUAL PERSPECTIVE: Belief in yourself can always be rekindled. Every moment is an opportunity to live up to new standards of accountability. Every decision is a fresh chance to take the high road. When you meditate or pray, fill yourself with an image of self-forgiveness. This could be a feminine energy such as Kuan-yin or Mother Mary, a teacher such as Jesus or Buddha, or even a simple warm light. Dotti Coon, proprietor of the busy website "Dotti's Weight Loss Zone" (www.dottisweightlosszone.com) knows all about the importance of beginning again. Her motto: "One day at a time, no guilt, and move on."

I'm Afraid of Failing

Everyone is afraid of failing. Some of us are afraid from the get-go, others are afraid of failing after we succeed (that's called fear of success). Even though we understand that successful ventures almost always follow several past failures, emotionally we still see failure as final — no second chance. It's almost a primitive fear. We'll do anything to avoid failing, even if it means never getting started.

Failure is nothing more than feedback; it's information. When you fail, you learn something. Next time, you'll have more data and a better chance at success. Of course, this is only so much intellectual mumbo jumbo until you put it into practice. Here are a few suggestions:

- *Reframe failure as a positive experience.* Failure means that you did something, you took a chance, you had courage, you didn't play it safe. As the saying goes, when you hit a speed bump, at least you know you're moving.

- *Remember that failure is relative.* I may feel bad because I failed to catch a fish, but the fish feels pretty successful. Even my most spectacular failures (oh, there were some good ones!) produced positive results somewhere down the road. Every failure contains the seeds of victory.

- *Rehearse success.* Determine which problems you're most likely to encounter and practice handling them successfully. Rehearsal is a standard stress-reduction technique used by speakers, athletes, and actors. Try practicing some of my favorite responses, such as, "So what?" "Who cares?" "Big deal." "Oh, well." "Go figure."

THE SPIRITUAL PERSPECTIVE: Everything fits inside God — even experiences like failure. All experiences have value. This perspective doesn't excuse bad behavior or discount negative events, but it does provide a context for handling them. When you make the decision to find a positive outcome, something wonderful can happen in the unseen.

I'm Too Old, Young, Disabled, Tired . . .

Some excuses masquerade as good reasons. For example, fifty years ago being physically disabled would have been a good excuse to avoid competitive sports. But today people with disabilities are encouraged to participate in many forms of physical activity. We even have the Paralympics, in which elite disabled athletes are judged by their achievements, not their limitations.

People allow all kinds of limitations to keep them from living large. They become what writer Spalding Grey calls "vicarians," living through others because they believe they can't do it themselves. Don't settle for being a vicarian. Life is too wonderful to limit. Tailor your goal to fit your capabilities. Start with small tasks, then gently, slowly, reach beyond your comfort zone. Find your edge and inch past it. You'll be amazed at what you can accomplish — and at the fun you'll have.

THE SPIRITUAL PERSPECTIVE: See yourself as a whole spiritual being, regardless of how limited you may feel. When you center yourself in a quiet frame of mind and consciously align yourself with infinite possibility, you'll find the courage to touch the edges of what can be. Because energy follows thought, your first small step toward a goal helps you take more and more steps in the same direction. You can go much farther than you think.

Goal-Setting Hints and Tips

Here are a few ideas to help you meet your goals with greater ease and less anxiety.

Identify a Grail

Most people seem to remember (and often relive) their tragic failures in greater detail than their stirring successes. This is especially unfortunate because energy always follows the dominant thought pattern. If your primary focus is on failure, guess what you'll probably continue to experience? You would be smarter to ponder your successes and stash the failures as reference material.

Years ago, I participated in an organization that promoted structured experiences they called "grails." A grail was an exceptionally challenging goal — the object of a difficult quest, an undertaking that taxed a person to the core. I realized that I didn't need to engineer a grail because my life was built on them: learning to walk, riding a two-wheeler, surviving high school, and recovering from relationship and health crises. Military boot camp is a classic grail experience, as is Outward Bound. Grails give us the opportunity to say, "If I can do that, I can do anything."

Take a look at your life and bring to mind a grail that you achieved — a big success. Think about the challenges and struggles you endured. If you can't find a grail in your repertoire of experience, then look at what you're working on now. You may have a grail in process. Keep the thought of your grail close to your heart because it is a strong magic. It reminds you in no uncertain terms of what you've already accomplished. It fuels belief in yourself and empowers you to persist. If you can do that, you can do anything.

Devise a Routine

Old, unhealthy habits are always ready to return. Sometimes it feels like everything and everyone is sabotaging your noble intentions. When you're tested by such forms of interference, your resolve can drain away. This is the time for a constructive routine to save the day.

For example, when I decided to start swimming regularly, I established a routine of packing my gym bag the night before, draping my swimsuit and sweats over the dresser, and storing my shoes next to the bed. When the alarm clock rang, I rolled out of bed, donned my swimsuit, sweats, and shoes, then headed out the door, gym bag in hand. I was in the car turning the ignition key before I thought to complain about it being so early in the morning.

I still have thoughts like, "Oh, just stay in bed one more hour." But my routine prevails because it's a habit; habit kicks in when the flesh is weak. I don't have to think much about it. If you are ready to tackle a goal, take a good look at the areas where you're most likely to blow it. Plan a routine to handle the negative influence, then practice it. A positive routine is one of your greatest allies.

Release and Redefine a Goal

When we decide on a goal, we must commit ourselves to it. Otherwise, why bother? On the other hand, as we progress down our path we may find that the goal needs to be adjusted or even released. We often grow beyond our goals. Yet some people cling to them like outdated hairstyles. ("Well, it used to look good on me.") We're afraid to set a new direction because it seems like we've already missed the mark.

When I was in college, my goal was to be a psychologist. As I neared completion of my degree work, I became distracted and bored. Graduate schools favored a research orientation that didn't interest me. I was a mediocre student. My goal seemed to fizzle. For a while, I felt like a failure. Then I realized that I needed to stop whining and create a new goal. I didn't have an ultimate career in mind, but I knew my strengths, so I became a technical writer and eventually a computer programmer. After many years, I redefined my goals and returned to writing. I take Anne Sullivan's words to heart:

> Keep on beginning and failing. Each time you fail, start all over again and you will grow stronger until you have accomplished a purpose — not the one you began with perhaps, but one you'll be glad to remember.

Expand Your Perspective

If you look closely at the area around your eyes, you'll likely see small lines and flaws, some inherited and others earned. It's easy to fixate on these imperfections if you keep staring at them. But if you step back, you'll notice that the imperfections work together to create your unique, special face.

Obstacles blocking your goal are like the imperfections of your skin. When you focus in too closely you'll lose your perspective and give the obstacles more influence than they probably merit. Instead, step back. Look around the issue and don't be so myopic; you're less likely to be derailed by it.

Stay Open at the Top

As you work toward a goal, whether it's the embodiment of a quality or the completion of a project, stay open about the end result. Yes, it's important to set specific, measurable goals; that's how you know when you've reached them. However, it's entirely possible that, no matter how carefully you strategize, your plans will steer you into unforeseen territory. If you keep your options open, you'll be able to respond quickly and proactively. When a plan goes awry, it may just mean there's something better cooking.

For example, a friend who was anxious to be a mother learned that her body wouldn't support pregnancy. Devastated but not destroyed, she decided that there was more than one way to start a family. She researched foster care, Big Sisters, and domestic and foreign adoption. Ultimately, she decided to adopt a child from China. "My world is bigger and brighter because of my daughter and her birth culture," she said. "What seemed like the end of the world was actually just the beginning." My friend stayed open even though she was hurting inside. She didn't shut down, and the result was better than anything she could have dreamed up herself. When you stay open at the top, you make room for miracles.

The Spiritual Practice

All goal-setting processes should be supported by daily meditation or prayer. Both practices can open your heart and teach you to hear the infinite. Both will transform goal-setting from a self-absorbed ritual into an openhearted evocation of universal creativity.

Prayer is a simple, elegant practice that varies from religion to religion. If you don't know how to pray but would like to learn, try reading *Prayer Is Good Medicine* by Dr. Larry Dossey or talk to your minister or rabbi about techniques.

I'm a big fan of meditation. There are countless books that describe how to establish a daily meditation practice. Some of my favorites are listed in appendix 1. In my book *Meditation for Busy People*, I offer an uncomplicated four-step system that incorporates prayer. Here's a summary:

Step 1: Relax

Sit in a comfortable position with your back supported. Avoid lying down, which makes you more likely to fall asleep. Either focus your eyes on the floor in front of your feet, or close them completely. Mentally sweep through your body, telling your muscles to relax. Take a few deep breaths and release all the air from your lungs, imagining the tension in your body flowing away with your outgoing breath. Allow your muscles to unwind and your hands to open. The idea is to minimize internal physical distractions as much as possible.

Step 2: Center Yourself

Using your breath as a focal point, find a place around your nostrils or the back of your breathing passages were you can feel the flow of air. Feel its temperature. Pay attention to each breathing cycle. If your mind wanders off into distraction, gently bring it back to your breathing. Don't become upset or angry with yourself. This isn't about force; it's about patience, tolerance, and — most of all — persistence.

Centering helps you delve into the spaces between your thoughts. In those spaces, you can find solutions to problems. Centering also cultivates mindfulness — the ability to witness what is going on without getting lost in it. When you're mindful, you stop behaving like a slave to habitual reactions and unconscious, counterproductive behavior; there's room in your heart for compassion, understanding, and new responses.

Step 3: Pray or Visualize

If you find comfort in prayer, this is an excellent time to do it. Your mind is settled and your body is quiet; you're primed for inspired thinking. You could also creatively visualize your goal being accomplished. Creative visualization involves imagining yourself experiencing completed goals or desired feelings. The key is to mentally use all your physical senses; whatever you're imagining, try to see, feel, taste, smell, hear, and touch it. Immerse yourself in it. You're making a blueprint of your desired experience in your mind.

Step 4: Release

Release is the wrap-up portion of your quiet time. It bridges the gap between meditative and everyday awareness levels. It also reinforces the entire experience, making subsequent sittings easier to approach. Simply take a very deep breath and begin to move your fingers and toes. This reconnects you with your body. Next, acknowledge yourself for having allowed this experience to take place. If your quiet time was rewarding and uplifting, that's great. If you were restless, distracted, or bored, that's okay, too. Observing all mental states teaches you how capricious they are. You can practice not taking them too seriously.

When to Set a Goal

There is some danger in overstating the importance of spiritual goal-setting. All of us experience times when we flow effortlessly with life. Many great achievements are intuitively guided. Many tasks can be completed without struggle. So when should you consider spiritual goal-setting as an option? Here are a few suggestions:

- When you want to do something, but never get around to it;

- When your blood pressure is rising from too many projects in the works;

- When your resistance to a goal increases as you near its completion;

- When you feel unmotivated about a goal;

- When you're frustrated because you seem to be repeating the same mistakes;

- When you're afraid to tackle something important because you might fail.

Spiritual goal-setting is a tool for dealing with resistance and challenge. If you're not experiencing resistance, then you don't need to do it. But if you're at your wits' end from slogging through stress, distraction, and meaninglessness, then spiritual goal-setting can make a difference.

▲▲▲

At some point in my life, I realized that no white knight was going to ride up and present me with a fit body and a happy mind. Stress wasn't going to just fade away on its own, and neither were my unhealthy habits. My life trajectory wasn't good. So I put one foot in front of the other. I decided that I didn't want to live with anxiety attacks, chronic health problems, and postponed happiness. I was sick and tired of it. Day by day, I started to make small changes in my behavior and my outlook.

I hope that by reading this book, you, too, will decide to make stress reduction a priority. You don't have to live in the hell of anxiety. There's a way through it. You can find peace in this chronically anxious world. If I can do it, anybody can do it. It may not be easy, but so what? Life is supposed to be challenging and interesting and full of surprises. There's no time like the present to start appreciating it.

"The place you are right now God circled on a map for you."

— Ibraham Hafiz

....

notes

Chapter 1

1   David B. Posen, M.D., "Stress Management for Patient and Physician," *Canadian Journal of Continuing Medical Education*, April 1995.

2   Edward M. Hallowell, M.D., *Worry: Controlling It and Using It Wisely* (New York: Pantheon Books, 1997).

3   The National Institute for Occupational Safety and Health, "Stress at Work, Publication No. 99–101" (Cincinnati, Ohio: NIOSH, 1999).

4   Hans Selye, *Stress without Distress* (Philadelphia: Lippincott Publishing, 1974).

5   National Institute of Mental Health, "Facts about Anxiety Disorders, Publication No. OM-99 4152" (Bethesda, Md.: NIMN, 1999).

6   Jon Kabat-Zinn, *Full Catastrophe Living: Using the Wisdom of Your Body and Mind to Face Stress, Pain, and Illness* (New York: Delacorte Press, 1990).

Chapter 2

7   Bo Lozoff, *It's a Meaningful Life: It Just Takes Practice* (New York: Penguin Group USA, 2001).

8   Harry Goldstein, "Resetting the Circadian Clock," *The Pennsylvania Gazette* 97, no. 5, (May–June 1999).

9   James B. Maas, *Power Sleep: The Revolutionary Program That Prepares Your Mind for Peak Performance* (New York: HarperPerennial, 1999).

10   S. E. Taylor, et al.,"Female Responses to Stress: Tend and Befriend, Not Fight or Flight," *Psychological Review* 107, no. 3 (2000): 419–429.

11   B. L. Fredickson, "Cultivating Positive Emotions to Optimize Health and Well-Being," *Prevention and Treatment* 3 (2000): article 1.

12   P. Ekman, R. J. Davidson, and W. V. Friesen, "The Duchenne Smile: Emotional Expression and Brain Physiology: II," *Journal of Personality and Social Psychology* 58 (1990): 342–353.

13   S. E. Snodgrass, J. G. Higgins, and L. Todisco, "The Effects of Walking Behavior on Mood" (paper presented at the 94th Annual Convention of the American Psychological Association, Washington, D.C., August 1986).

14   Dharma Singh Khalsa, M.D., *Meditation As Medicine: Activate the Power of Your Natural Healing Force* (New York: Simon & Schuster, 2002).

15   The findings of these studies can be viewed at the website of Duke's Center for the Study of Religion/Spirituality and Health, http://www.dukespiritualityandhealth.org/research.html.

16   Dr. Larry Dossey, M.D., "Can Spirituality Improve Your Health?" *Bottom Line Secrets,* July 1, 2001, http://www.bottomlinesecrets.com/.

Chapter 4

17   Shunryu Suzuki Roshi, *Zen Mind, Beginner's Mind* (New York: Walker/Weatherhill, 1970).

18   Edward Said, *Beginnings: Intention and Method* (New York: Columbia University Press, 1987).

appendix 1

....

recommended reading

Books

The Dalai Lama and Howard C. Cutler, M.D. *The Art of Happiness at Work*. New York: Riverhead Books, 2003.

Dossey, Larry, *Prayer Is Good Medicine: How to Reap the Healing Benefits of Prayer*. San Francisco: Harper San Francisco, 1997. This book examines how prayer can induce optimal healing benefits, regardless of spiritual discipline.

Gordhamer, Soren. *Just Say Om! Your Life's Journey*. Avon, Mass.: Adams Media Corporation, 2001. An accessible introduction to meditation and yoga for children and teens.

Groves, Dawn. *Massage for Busy People: Five Minutes to a More Relaxed Body*. Novato, Calif.: New World Library, 1999.

————. *Meditation for Busy People: 60 Seconds to Serenity*. Novato, Calif.: New World Library, 1993.

————. *Yoga for Busy People: Increase Energy and Reduce Stress in Minutes a Day*. Novato, Calif.: New World Library, 1995.

Hallowell, Edward M., M.D. *Worry: Controlling It and Using It Wisely*. New York: Random House, 1998. An interesting, practical, accessible book about managing worry in your life.

Kabat-Zinn, Jon. *Full Catastrophe Living: Using the Wisdom of Your Body and Mind to Face Stress, Pain, and Illness*. New York: Delacorte

Press, 1990. A complete stress-reduction manual that explains the program successfully used in the Stress Reduction Clinic at the University of Massachusetts Medical Center.

Khalsa, Dharma Singh, M.D. *Meditation As Medicine: Activate the Power of Your Natural Healing Force.* New York: Simon & Schuster, 2002. An exciting book about the uses of meditation, yoga, and breathing techniques in healing.

Lasater, Judith, Ph.D., P.T. *Relax and Renew: Restful Yoga for Stressful Times.* Berkeley, Calif.: Rodmell Press, 1995. An excellent book on using yoga to reduce stress.

Lozoff, Bo. *It's a Meaningful Life: It Just Takes Practice.* New York: Penguin, 2001. A powerful, practical, no-nonsense work about living with heart.

MacGilchrist, Colleen and Bob. *Match! Simple Strategies for Happily Ever After.* Bellingham, Wash.: Abintra Publishing, 2003. A wise, entertaining little book with some great ideas about relationships.

Salzberg, Sharon. *Loving-Kindness Meditation: Learning to Love through Insight Meditation.* Boston: Shambhala Publications, 2002. A powerful book for both beginning and experienced meditators.

———. *Lovingkindness: The Revolutionary Art of Happiness.* Boston: Shambhala Publications, 1997.

Weil, Andrew, M.D. *Eating Well for Optimum Health: The Essential Guide to Bringing Health and Pleasure Back to Eating.* New York: HarperCollins, 2001. A thorough, motivating manual for taking back your health through proper eating.

Magazines

Simple Living Magazine
Yoga Journal Magazine

appendix 2

·····································

common questions

....

about the author

Dawn Groves is a minister, author, and educator who clearly addresses the challenges of people attempting to combine professional achievement, spiritual growth, and a balanced lifestyle. She teaches workshops and classes for the government, private industry, community colleges, and spiritual centers throughout the United States and Canada. She is the author of *Meditation for Busy People, Massage for Busy People,* and *Yoga for Busy People.*

For information about Dawn's lectures, workshops, classes, and tapes, please visit her website:

www.dawngroves.com

New World Library is dedicated to
publishing books and audio products
that inspire and challenge us to improve
the quality of our lives and our world.

Our products are available
in bookstores everywhere.
For our catalog, please contact:

New World Library
14 Pamaron Way
Novato, California 94949

Phone: (415) 884-2100 or (800) 972-6657
Catalog requests: Ext. 50
Orders: Ext. 52
Fax: (415) 884-2199

Email: escort@newworldlibrary.com
Website: www.newworldlibrary.com